REGULAR
GRAPHIC
DESIGN
TODAY

gestalten

BP45

GUILLAUME CHUARD / ECAL

Library Sign System

Library sign system based on the principle of
tags. Like in a web forum, users can ask and
answer questions with bookmarks. If a book
is the subject of many discussions, it will be
noticeable from afar.

12/20/10

FRANÇOIS RAPPO (b.1955) is a graphic designer and typographer living and working in Lausanne, Switzerland. He is the head of the Graphic Design Department at ECAL (Ecole cantonale d'art de Lausanne), and is the author of numerous typefaces such as Didot Elder, Genath, LaPolice, New Fournier and Theinhardt Grotesk. Rappo has also served as Chair of The Most Beautiful Swiss Books Prize from 2001 to 2007.

GRAPHIC FICTION

BY FRANÇOIS RAPPO

For some time in the 1990s, there was a graphic design supported and accompanied by narratives, fictions and by a 'new discourse'. Discourses of teachers, of journalists and of designers too; discourses that, with time, became a chorus, or from today's perspective something like a paradigm – a paradigm, that moment when the eggs in a pan begin to firm up and become something else, the moment they become an omelette. Not too much though. It's a paradigm that ratified, as it did earlier in several other fields, the label of 'postmodern' in graphic design. A paradigm of the 1990s. I organised my bookshelf. For the books on design, I happily use a classification based on the table of contents of Wikipedia's article on 'Science Fiction': Hard, Soft & Social, Cyberpunk, Time Travel, Alternate History, Military SF, Superhuman, Apocalyptic, Space Opera, Space Western, Superhero, Awards, Fanzines and Online Fiction, etc. Graphic design and Sci-Fi; it's the same thing today. Easy to classify: an interview with Sheila Levrant de Bretteville, with Paolo Portoghesi, Martin Jay, Rick Poynor, P. Scott Makela, and also four copies of *Schiff nach Europa* by Karl Gerstner. I employ the same model to create a mind map of the current scene of graphic design.

Graphic design has been particularly, perhaps exceptionally, receptive to the themes of the period: mass culture, sub-culture, context, aesthetics of reception and connection. Perhaps professional culture, the academic models, the discussions on graphic design, were particularly permeable to this Zeitgeist. Much more so than architecture. A little bit like pop music? Which makes us ask ourselves: is graphic design an autonomous zone? To what degree? Is it 'hardcore', centred on itself, as it could have been, let's say, forty years ago? Or is it immersed in mass culture and consequently today the beneficiary of a particular experience resulting from this mix?

But it is difficult to summarise the discourse on graphic design today. Graphic design is still too fragmented. That said, there has been a turning point, new observations, which, according to the passage of time, are more perceptible. Thus, having been adduced as an argument, it is perceptible that mass culture is not any less tautological than high culture. The postmodern 'friendly designer', invested in the relational, miming his or her client (his or her table companion) also seems a participant in strategies of reified communication or the growing influence of communication techniques on immediate experience and the spontaneity of the everyday. The mediatisation of design these past years, which has passed as much by the persona, the individual, the designer, as by its signature, leaves us to suspect that there is an attempt to make up for the wearing out of old beliefs and possibly an added use value brought through design.

The bride stripped naked by her bachelors, even? The expansion of design this decade occurred around three synchronised events, like three graphical layers that are superimposed: a layer of postmodern aesthetics, cultural studies, gay and lesbian studies, poststructuralism; a political layer, neo-liberalism and new subjectivities; a sociological layer, the advancement of education, the achievement of design, the achievement of schools of design. 'The *grand tour* for the masses'. The relevance of design is its success.

HARD
SOFT & SOCIAL
CYBERPUNK
TIME TRAVEL
ALTERNATE HISTORY
MILITARY SF
SUPERHUMAN
APOCALYPTIC
SPACE OPERA
SPACE WESTERN
SUPERHERO
AWARDS
FANZINES AND
ONLINE FICTION
...

The key to this period, the gangway for new actors as well, was the 'pomo' aesthetic that has been frequently cited, borrowed and translated. What has it left, now that everyone believes that it has become a rather tired concept? In my library, this yields a greater frame of reference on questions of meaning, on the context of reception, a flexible matrix to try to cross these variables with specific graphical languages, in the context of a period of use. Perhaps it is an innovative possibility to think of the relationship between specialised / mass culture. It is the ability to anticipate. Have not the majority of 'pomo''s promises remained unfulfilled, stayed in their own particular niches? This in itself does not disqualify them, but how can one imagine a map of these niches in order to grasp the current debate? A flexible map that covers the surface of the 'long tail' of the net. There, graphic design, in this case, has become a new murmuring discourse, categories like Superhero and Fan fiction, a showroom and an infinite buzz. I am looking for the motor of mental research that permits one to find new and relevant 'loops'. But that circulation of ideas has become more complicated, as the loop must have a minimum of effect in order to situate itself in some location, in the city or the country, here like elsewhere –isn't that the case? And in that loop, it is necessary to know how to distinguish its own traces from those of others. I have often travelled the 'neo-conceptualist' loop. A showroom of critical design, dry and austere, very 'niched', procedural: auto-publication, editions and conferences,

protected communication (academies, galleries); exploring a vernacular culture of conceptual art of the 70s, citing flyers, catalogue posters, typographies themselves, 'for lack of anything better'. A high culture loop in this case. I also travel through a 'neo-graphical' loop. Grotesque Fandom: look, grampa and grandma did it like that, 'shave-up metrics', the buzz of Helvetica and of erudition. The loop of enchanted patrimony and of legitimate filiation. In this loop, most recently, two catalogue covers by Franciszka Themerson for *Cybernetic Serendipity*, scripting, numerical collage and typewriter font, ICA, 1968 – the language of today. I am also, in parallel, in a loop, 'design around the corner'. Here, it is not industrial and it is not design. If it's not massive, then it's a private correspondence illegitimately mixed with the space. Corporate design, brand, services. If possible, design should be here, please! Anonymous, or only that of an agency. Better: internal. My, your, street corner: you pass, a glance, it's transparent, you pick up pace. My best loop is that of magazines and fanzines, the classification breaks down here. I think sometimes today that all affirmation, discourse, statement, should be verified, at least mentally, on the model of a magazine, ephemeral and from a moment. By its editorial stance and its artistic direction. The magazine is the true graphic medium of these past years. An interesting and paradoxical materiality, a good sense of connectivity with other media, a real ground for play. In its corner, it might be an excellent power aggregate, better than industrial ones.

Because the practice of bringing together, this aggregate, finds itself at a superior level to that of the loop! In fact, the themes of the postmodern catalogue are not going to weaken, but will be redistributed to a landscape of our aggregates, to new themes. I think that the 'rationalist' themes take on new visibility, incorporate new desires, around profiles, information, scripting, 'copy left' or 'grotesque' typographical style. The relations overflow from their context to reach their critical potential, through elaboration and formalisation. And, why not a little taste of rationality?

But the aggregate of aggregates puts into the question the very image of the space, stretched between a group of specific fields: photography, illustration, typography (non-limited enumeration) and the vacillating competence of the graphic designer. Only the new paradigm, if one needs it, the new omelette which is about to firm, permits, dear reader, the imperfect but substantial understanding of the new Zeitgeist. Something which builds a bridge to a history that is slower than it is murmuring?

It's done, I pack up my library.

François Rappo, May 2009

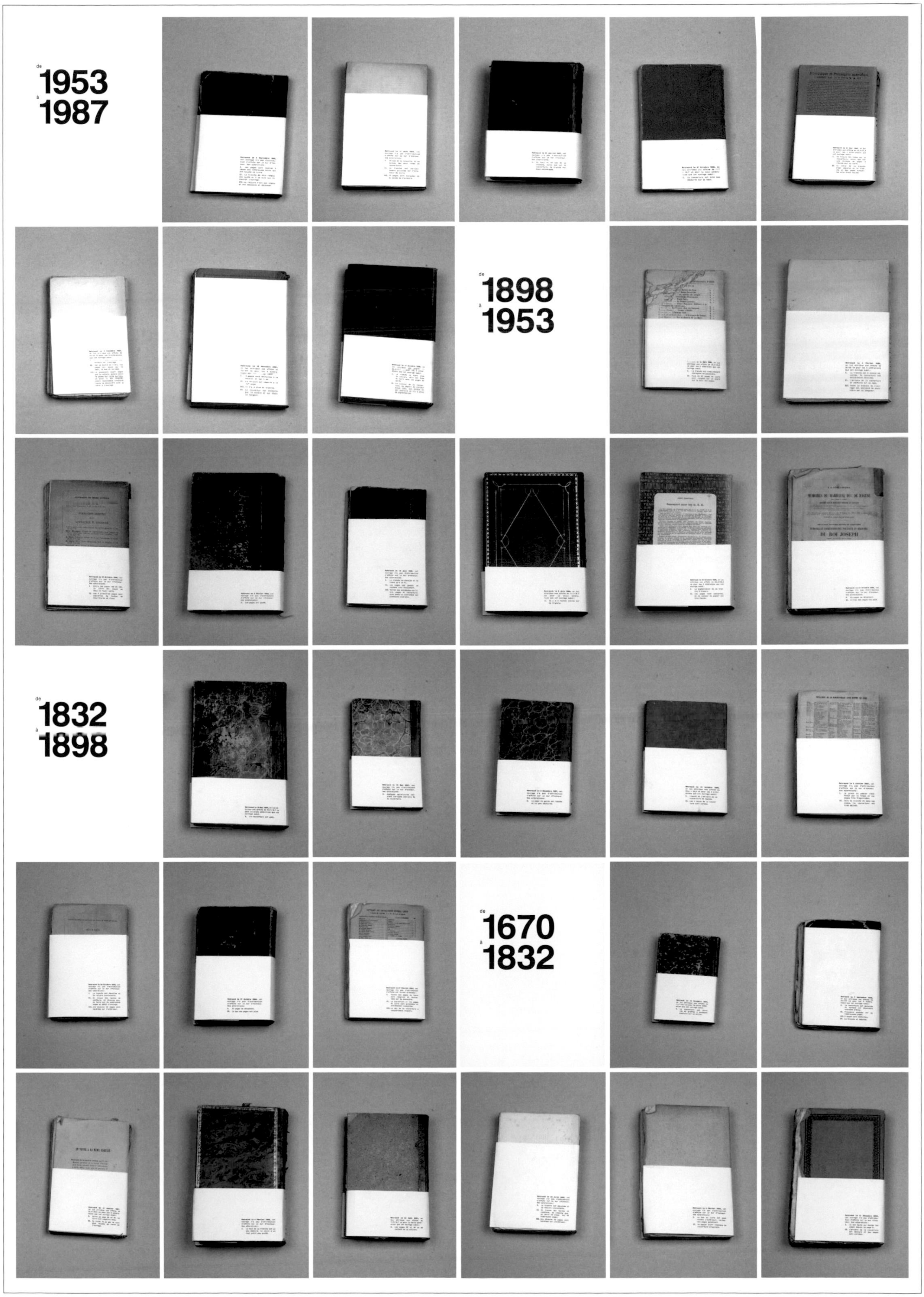

de **1953**
à **1987**

de **1898**
à **1953**

de **1832**
à **1898**

de **1670**
à **1832**

REGULAR /
DADA

BY
ROBERT
KLANTEN

This is a book about current conventional graphic design and about the contemporary designers who are creating the basis today for what we will consider as graphic design tomorrow. At the end of the first decade of the new millennium, design is being strongly influenced by three main factors: digitalisation, materialisation and personalisation / identity.

When one speaks of classic graphic design, the continental European school of design in countries such as Switzerland, the Netherlands and Germany is generally what is meant. Anglo-Saxon design, which principally refers to design from Great Britain and the USA, has always had little in common with the contextual understanding of design that applies in continental Europe. Instead, Anglo-Saxon design is more image-oriented and operates in a mercilessly pragmatic manner, following the motto 'F**k the concept – let's make something funny!'

There are many reasons for this, but the main reason appears to be that the Anglo-Saxon school of design has its roots in the rupture in the understanding of art that occurred in the 1920s. Beforehand, both sides of the Atlantic had been singing on the same page during the Impressionist years; however, after the First World War, an alternative perception of such conceptual and utopian visions of Art Nouveau, Constructivism, Futurism, Surrealism, Expressionism and Dada led America and Britain down a different path.

DEMAND
VISUAL CULTURE
DEMOCRATISATION
TRANSITION
SIEGE

...

These artistic movements shaped people's understanding of art and artistry in Latin-influenced countries and in Russia from here on; at the same time, American Realism developed in North America, which eventually lead to pop culture and to Pop Art which still dominate imagery today. The worldwide exchange of images that takes place nowadays means that clearly defined stylistic classifications no longer exist. There are still regional design traditions and works which can be identified as typical, but the globalisation of contemporary graphic design has also resulted in the establishment of an international style. Works that are created in Brazil and Spain, Japan and Korea, or in Scandinavia, for example, may use elements of American / Anglo-Saxon imagery while of course also borrow from continental European design. In addition, local traditions will also influence the use of colours, fonts and images. Anything goes, and regional stylistic rules are no longer important.

The increasing digitalisation of design since the 1990s has also led to a process of democratisation in design. With the advent of desktop publishing, graphic design technology has become accessible to almost anyone, and the relevant skills can be acquired from readily available manuals and sets of instructions. At the same time, images and symbols, which are the raw materials for every graphic design, are being digitalised, copied and sold at low prices. There is no limit to the reproducibility of digital image contents, and fonts, images and graphic programs are freely available. In principle, you only need a computer with an Internet connection and a little bit of criminal energy in order to do graphics yourself.

Graphic design is no longer as elitist as it was back in the 1960s and 1970s, when the discipline still had an aura of craftsmanship attached to it. The democratisation of design has not yet led to an implosion in the sector for the sole reason that the demand for visual design has risen in inverse proportion to the drop in prices. In the 1970s, perhaps a few dozen or a few hundred fonts were being published each year, each of which had been worked on for months or for years by designers; nowadays, the figure is of the order of tens of thousands, and most of these fonts are available for a fraction of what fonts used to cost.

Graphic design is currently going through a phase similar to that experienced by pop music back in the 1990s, when it became possible to produce electronic / contemporary music at home thanks to inexpensive and easy-to-use samplers and sequencers. Everyone can do it and everyone is doing it! The results and the commercial success of designs are no longer dependent on learning how to use technology and how to practice a trade; instead, they hinge mainly on the mastery of visual codes. These visual codes are, in turn, the result of technical advancements and the social consequences of these advancements – for example, consider hyperreal photography, which has resulted from the mass availability of digital cameras.

The end of 'elitist' design and of specialisations has lead to a more multi-disciplinary environment. Young designers are often also active as graphic designers, video producers, type designers, illustrators, artists, musicians or event managers. At a time when graphic design is so clearly under siege, it is only natural that graphic design itself should react to this. *Regular: Graphic Design Today* examines graphic design as a classic design discipline, as a conceptional starting point for design and the transmission of information, and, last but not least, as an element of overall visual culture.

DIGITALISATION

Graphic design certainly has a new image of itself, even though the tasks and topics that come under the umbrella of graphic design haven't changed significantly. Typography, editorial design, poster design and other conventional applications are deliberately dealt with in this book not in neatly separated chapters, but rather in terms of clusters which are interlinked and flow from one topic into the next.

Alongside the process of democratisation mentioned at the beginning, the traditional graphic design task of directly transmitting information has become obsolete. A lot of the information that traditionally used to be conveyed by newspapers, magazines and posters has now migrated to the Internet, and is instead communicated in blogs and newsfeeds. The invention of photography in the 19th century freed naturalist landscape and portrait painting from its traditional task of representation, thus clearing the way for Impressionism and its very personal, subjective perception; in the same manner, analogue media and graphic design which shapes these media now also have different functions in the present phase of transition.

REFUSAL
CARTE BLANCHE
EPHEMERAL
SLASH / SLASH
UTOPIAS
DEDICATION

...

transient design – as demonstrated by the works of a designer like Marije Vogelzang: "Originally I am a product designer, but I chose food as my material. I like the fact that my design is eaten and then it's gone. It's ephemeral." However, the use of material and the emphasis on material is not just a central issue in graphic design; this is demonstrated by the New Craft movement, where the protagonists employ manual and craft skills such as knitting and glass-blowing. Thus in many areas, the particular attraction of the tactile design of a product or piece of art lies in the fact that you can see from the resulting piece that it has been produced not industrially, but instead by a real human designer or artist. The design reflects the human time and dedication that has been invested in it – things which are valuable in themselves.

MATERIALISATION / EXTENSION OF MATERIAL

The fact that analogue media (for example, the telephone book) no longer have to fulfil their primary task of providing up-to-date information because this information has moved to the Internet also means that analogue media now have more freedom. Instead, magazines, daily newspapers and posters have taken on new functions: they help to classify and give context to the unfiltered flow of current information. In this way, the information becomes personalised, consumable, and thus valuable. With the advent of digitalisation, material has actually gained in status, as material is binding and more weighty.

Materialisation is thus a major issue. Designers attempt to use non-reproducible experiences and tactile creations outside the realm of computers in order to create something that cannot be copy-and-pasted. Material and space cannot simply be transmitted over a telephone wire. An aura of authenticity and of realness is attached to material, and to odour and taste too, in a manner that doesn't apply to sounds and images. Designers create installations and atmospheres in order to create a very personal impression on observers or visitors. Even though this impression is meant to be permanent, the design itself need not exist forever. Atmosphere and a personal signature can also be achieved by metaphorical,

IDENTITY

Graphic design today finds itself located somewhere between new design freedoms on the one hand, and more difficult economic conditions on the other hand. The logical consequence of this is the effort to create a strong identity. The initial defensive reaction to popularisation and democratisation is one of hermetic isolationism. Analogous to the *Diskurspop* movement in German music in the late 80s and early 90s, today one can also speak of 'discursive graphics'. The creation of higher complexities has always been a feature of every evolution, and aesthetic fragmentation is associated with this. In the 1990s and the first decade of the new millennium, designers generally gave their works two stylistic features or tags and combined disciplines (such as photography with illustration, typography with illustration, or typography with installation) in order to create works of increased complexity. Nowadays, designers like to combine three different stylistic tools – for example photography, typography and patterns – to create complex works.

At the end of the 1990s, designers began to superimpose awkward sketches on photographs and used trivial ballpoint-pen drawings in an attempt to 'humanise' the sober vector graphics and the hyperreal photo aesthetics that were dominant at the time. This is well summed up by the stereotypical manner of presentation of posters today where the posters are held in front of the camera by the designers themselves and captured in photography. This gesture underlines the need for humanisation, personalisation and identity in graphic design. This image metaphor says: "Even though you can't see me, there is still a real person behind this piece."

Today, graphic designers also try to make their works more productive and lend them greater value by reducing the superficiality of these works. One way of achieving this is to remove the traditional surfaces from magazines and books by placing the table of contents right on the cover.

'Authorship' means that designers are no longer just laying out content supplied by external sources, but instead are increasingly creating all the components of their designs (images, fonts) themselves. This happens to such an extent that posters, small portfolios and magazines are being produced and published entirely by the designers themselves. Many designers have bought a 'Risograph' for just this purpose: roughly speaking, this device combines photocopying with screen printing, and allows users to change the ink cartridges and use special colours. Pieces produced in this manner often have a typical, but unusual colour feel, as they are not based on the standardised CMYK scale used in offset printing. These personal works are reproduced on the Risograph and then bound. The resulting portfolios and magazines around a single subject are produced in small numbers, and are often distributed by the designers themselves using the Internet or by post, or are sent to or given as presents to clients.

Between the twin poles of commercial work and authorship, works are being created today that do not bring the designers any great financial rewards, but nonetheless allow them to develop their own design profile, thanks to an artistic *carte blanche* from clients, without the designers having to make too many compromises. These personal works then find their way into the designers' portfolios, which they can then use to compete for more lucrative contracts. Sometimes this works the other way around: commercial clients approach designers based on their personal works because the clients wish to use some element of this personal identity in their own commercial works. The targeted ideal is a 'signature collection' where designers are employed not despite, but rather because of their own trademark approach.

___

GENERIC / GLITCH

This type of deliberately anti-innovative pose can be seen in various design disciplines, as generic design is felt to be unassailable. On the one hand, basic forms of design are being sought: the image elements that have always been a part of human communication. First it was coats of arms and heraldic motifs such as dragons and gryphons, skulls, crosses, lightning, then spirals and alchemical motifs; and then came basic geometrical shapes such as circles, triangles, rectangles and other patterns. The colours used correspond to the CMYK scale or the colour wheel.

In recent years, young designers are borrowing neo-conservative, conventional, explicit design and stylistic tools which are clearly not particularly innovative. They use design stereotypes, and employ fonts such as Helvetica, Frutiger, the Signpainter and Stroke fonts of the 1950s, and space-age fonts such as Moonbase.

What is human is real, and that which features mistakes and refusals is considered human. In recent times, these conventional graphic design concepts have been deliberately altered as part of a rupture whose goal is to be as personal as possible. The design is given a certain texture in order to grant it a personal, analogue aura. Mistakes are included in order to attract attention. For example, parts of the text may be deleted, crossed-through or partially missing. Text is set diagonally or in wave patterns. Small irritants are included, and the impression is created that a finished design has been altered by another designer or some unknown censor. Misusing equipment also has its own aesthetic appeal – this was true even before Jimi Hendrix started abusing his electric guitar. In the same way that today's musicians superimpose the analogue crackling of vinyl records on top of their own computer-generated music, graphic designers add textures to sober computer graphics using exchangeable neo-conservative forms. Personal identity is formed by employing the concepts of refusal, irritation and deletion.

Particularly noticeable are the parallels between graphic design today and the major aesthetic cultural movement of rejection and doubt, namely Dada. Dadaism stood for universal doubt, radical individualism, and the complete refusal and rejection of aesthetic or societal categorisation. In contrast with the societal Utopias of Futurism and Constructivism which were present at the time, the Dadaists rejected all forms of pragmatism and social consensus. Instead, the Dadaists elevated chance and the resulting phenomena of refusal, deletion, nonsense and meaninglessness to the level of an aesthetic principle; they declared chance the single constant in human existence.

Alongside Surrealism and Expressionism, Dada was the most radical and individualistic counter-movement against the holistic aesthetic Utopias of the industrial age, namely Futurism and Constructivism. It seems appropriate today to refer back to Dada, which originally emerged during a time of upheaval and of global economic crisis around ninety years ago. Doubt and refusal are certainly capable of capturing the current state of affairs in an accurate and aesthetically exciting manner; but they will not solve today's problems. Inevitably, one asks oneself what the Dadaists, those most radical of rejecters, would have said to the adoption of their principles by today's imitators...

LUDOVIC BALLAND

Ludovic Balland was born in Geneva, Switzerland in 1973. Educated at the Schule für Gestaltung (School of Art and Design), Basel, Balland graduated with the equivalent of a master's degree in 2000. He set up his own studio, under the name Typographic Cabinet, in 2005, also in Basel. While the majority of Balland's work encompasses design books and posters for architects and cultural institutions, he is occasionally also commissioned to create identities. His prestigious client list includes Vitra, the Museum of Modern Art, Warsaw and Basel-based architects Herzog & de Meuron. Today Balland is assisted by designer Natacha Kirchner.

With a keen interest in Russian history since his school days, Balland was impressed at an early age by the power of Russian propaganda posters. In particular, he was always fascinated he says by "the beauty of the Cyrillic alphabet and Russian texts", adding: "I read poems by Majakowski and knew then that working with letters would one day be my job."

True to this thought, Balland's work today is mostly typographic in nature. "Typography in my eyes is the orchestration of different information in a defined format. So it's a question of proportion and relation between the forms the information relates to. This is about the sound of the composed text."

"For the visualisation," he continues, "I try to consider the text as different grey values: if you want, you could say I compare the composed text with a black and white photograph of the desert by Lee Friedlander, whom I consider one of the most important artists in the last century."

Balland also cites the early works of seminal designer and typographer Wolfgang Weingart as an inspiration.

His dream job? To re-design a newspaper. "Preferably *The New York Times*," he adds with a smile.

LUDOVIC BALLAND
TYPOGRAPHY CABINET

[01] Stadtkino Basel / Cineclub, January 2009

[02] Stadtkino Basel / Cineclub, October 2008

[03] Stadtkino Basel / Cineclub, November 2008

Series of posters for a cineclub showing a monthly distinctive selection of films. The information is set like news and refers to newspaper posters. The selected images are chosen and composed in an associative way, and together create new analogies.

Client Stadtkino, Basel

[01]

[02]

November

STADTKINO BASEL LANDKINO

SÉLECTION LE BON FILM:
WEISSE LILIEN
20. BIS 29. NOVEMBER

PROGRAMMPREIS DER
DEFA-STIFTUNG
24. BIS 30. NOVEMBER

ZWISCHEN ORIENT UND OKZIDENT

YILMAZ GÜNEY, NURI BILGE CEYLAN
UND DAS TÜRKISCHE KINO

À PROPOS DE VIGO

UNE MORAL DE LIBERTÉ ET
DE L'AMOUR

[04|05]

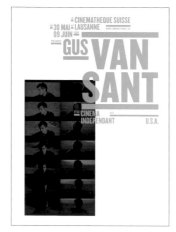

—
MARC BALLY / ECAL

[01]   Road Movie

[04]   Gus Van Sant

[05]   Futur Immédiat

Poster for the Swiss Film Archive.

—
GIAN BESSET

[02]   Modeschau

Poster for the 2008 diploma show of the
fashion design department of the Academy
of Art and Design Basel, Switzerland.

—
COBOI
Katharina Reidy

[03]   Kaki King & 2 Foot Yard

Poster for the Bad Bonn concert Hall in
Düdingen, Switzerland.

KAKI KING

HER GUITAR AND EDDIE VEDDER'S VOICE↓ INTO THE WILD

2 FOOT YARD

ROYAL POP ODER KAMMERMUSIK FOR THE STREET

Bad Bonn Düdingen
23.03.2009 → 21h

www.badbonn.ch

A Michael Kuhn presentation, by arrangement
with Primary Talent International

caboi

ZAK KLAUCK

[01] Terry Richardson

Poster based on the work of photographer
Terry Richardson.

Credits Photography by Terry Richardson

DENNY BACKHAUS

[02] Rietveld Yearbook 2008 Poster

Client Gerry Strawfield
Credits Photography by Janneke van Leeuwen

[03] Rietveld Prom 2008

Poster for the first annual Rietveld Prom
Night, organized by the Gerry Strawfield team.

Client Gerry Strawfield

[01]

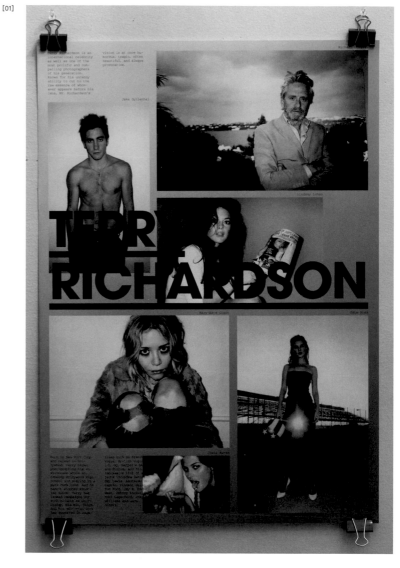

[02]

[03]

ZAT04APR
DE KIFT
& SUPPORT HELLSONGS (ZW)
Kassa Open: 20.00 Aanvang: 20.30
Entree: 12 euro

Poppodium EKKO, Bemuurde Weerd WZ 3, Utrecht www.ekko.nl   EKKO

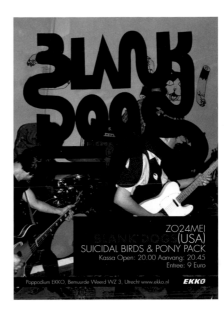

ZO24MEI
(USA)
SUICIDAL BIRDS & PONY PACK
Kassa Open: 20.00 Aanvang: 20.45
Entree: 9 Euro

Poppodium EKKO, Bemuurde Weerd WZ 3, Utrecht www.ekko.nl   EKKO

—
STUDIOSPASS
Jaron Korvinus & Daan Mens

[01–02] EKKO Promotional printworks

—
EMMANUEL REY & CLÉMENT GALLET

[03] Atlantic poster June 2008

Promotion for a theatre, cinema and
music space.

Client L'Atlantic, Bar & Spectacle

—
ZAK KLAUCK

[04] Rome Prize Poster

This poster was designed using a sticker
label system. The label acted as a violator,
drawing attention to the information and
away from the artwork.

Client American Academy in Rome
Credits Creative Direction by Michael Rock, 2x4

[03]

[04]

—
MAUREEN MOOREN
Oppression & Compassion

Posters for the Holland Festival 2007
Client Holland Festival

—
POSTERS

The conception and layout of posters is considered one of the conventional design disciplines. Poster design traditionally serves as a field of experimentation used by graphic designers, artists, illustrators, typographers and painters alike, where they can make their mark in a lively area of design and explore the limits of design freedom. Typography and calligraphy play an important role as formative visual elements, and strong, central motifs are also taken from the areas of photography, illustration and painting and integrated contextually.

Even though the design of posters gives precedence to creative experimentation and painstaking investigation, it is still based on clear principles. 'Vertical' narration is an inherent part of posters, as the observer is always able to see all components simultaneously. Differentiation is based on the distance from which the poster is seen. Font sizes and design elements are positioned at various intervals along the observation axis. When part of an urban landscape, posters are a combination of visual stimulation and an information medium – a juicy worm and a sharp hook cast out by designers in the direction of their observers. For this reason, an interesting issue is whether and how designers deal with this traditional method of 'drawing' observers' attention to the information contained in the poster; in other words, whether they grant more importance to making information visible than to the artistic urge, whether they take into account the fleeting manner in which posters are perceived, or whether they ignore poster conventions and simply treat them are large, homogeneous surfaces. In this case, they are the ideal playground for personal projects where authorship is manifested both in the poster's self-portraying design and in the fact that many one-off limited editions are printed and published by the designers themselves, and often enjoy the advantage of being aimed at an audience of visually-trained observers.

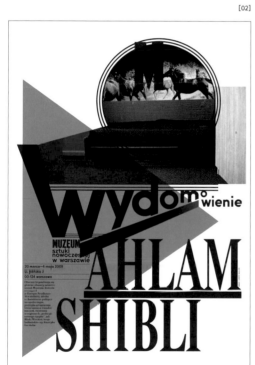

LUDOVIC BALLAND
TYPOGRAPHY CABINET

[01] Sztuka Cenniejsza Niz Zloto

Poster for the acquisition of the first collection of the Museum of Modern Art in Warsaw under the title: *Art More Precious than Gold.*

Client Museum of Modern Art in Warsaw

[02] Ahlam Shibli—Wydomowienie
Museum of Modern Art in Warsaw

Poster for the exhibition of the photographer Ahlam Shibli Wydomowienie *at the Museum of Modern Art* in Warsaw.

Client Museum of Modern Art in Warsaw

GIACOMO SANTIAGO ROGADO

FIRST

SECOND

Kunstmuseum Luzern 6.3.–14.6.09 Museum of Art Lucerne

PATIENCE

MANOR KUNSTPREIS LUZERN 2009

DO–SO 10–17H, MI 10–20H
28.3.–21.6. MO–SO 10–18H

Ausschreibung:
WERKBEITRÄGE 2008

Kanton und Stadt Luzern vergeben dieses Jah
PERFORMATIVE WORT- ODER LITER
Einge

WWW

[04|05]

CULTURA ANIMI

FIRST
GIACOMO
SECOND
SANTIAGO
PATIENCE
ROGADO
15.3.09
14H
KUNSTMUSEUM
LUZERN

ÜBERGABE
WERK
13.12.08 – 17H
BEI-
SUDPOL
TRÄGE
LUZERN

—
C2F
Cybu Richli & Fabienne Burri

[01]   First Second Patience –

Giacomo Santiago Rogado

Poster for an exhibition of the artist
Giacomo Santiago Rogado.

Client Museum of Art Lucerne

[02]   Contribution for tender 2008

Poster.

Client Kulturförderung Kanton und Stadt Luzern

[03]   Focused

Poster for the Design Research Symposium
2008 in Bern.

Client Swiss Design Network

[04]   Cultura Animi

Poster for the exhibition First Second
Patience.

Client Cultura Animi

[05]   Werkbeiträge 2008 Übergabe

Client Kulturförderung Kanton und Stadt Luzern

Posters for musical events that are designed with self-made tools.All the tools
and the process are based on the combination of manual and automatic tasks.

[05]

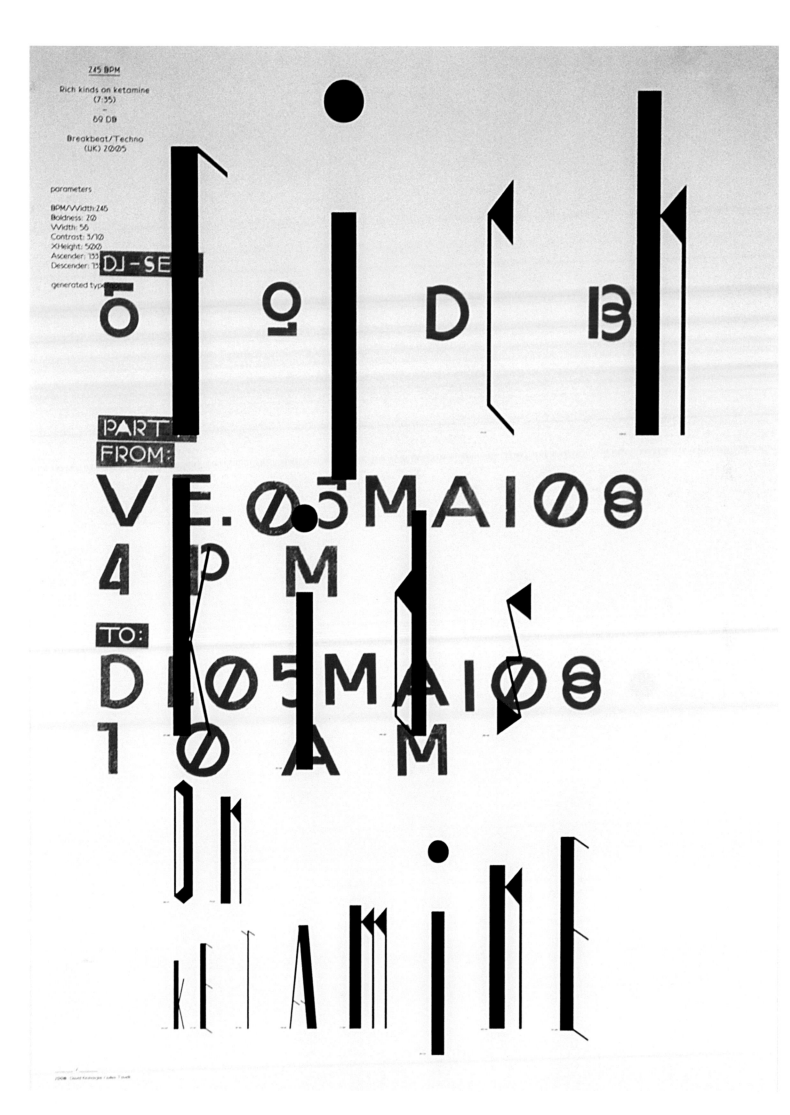

[01]

—
MAUREEN MOOREN

[01]   Serenity & Anxiety

        Poster for Holland Festival 2009.

[02]   If I Can't Dance,
        I Don't Want To Be Part Of Your Revolution

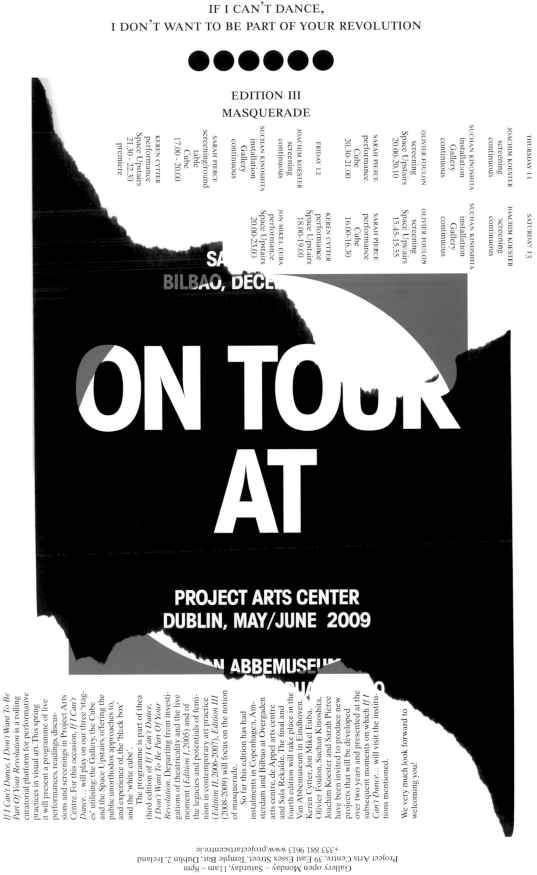

  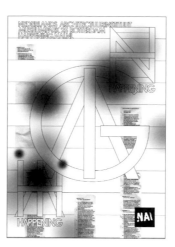

METAHAVEN
P. 24 – 25, 267

Metahaven are Dutch designer Daniel van der Velden, born in Rotterdam in 1971; designer Vinca Kruk, also Dutch but born in Leiden in 1980; and Israeli designer/architect Gon Zifroni, born in Askelon in 1980. and now based in Brussels, Belgium.

Launched in 2006, and based in Amsterdam and Brussels, *Metahaven* describe themselves as "a design research collective".

Their work connects graphic design and architecture, and is concerned with their political and ideological interdependencies. Explains Van der Velden: "By research, the group implies a gathering of data, inquiry, imagination and ultimately, speculation, which communicates their work in graphic design, branding and iconography as well as in architecture."

Projects to date include creating the visual identity for the Principality of Sealand, a mini-state, situated on a former anti-aircraft tower in the North Sea. The fortress was built in World War II to help defend the British Isles against an upcoming German invasion, but by 1946 the tower was abandoned by the British armed forces. The structure was squatted in 1967 by an Englishman, Roy Bates, and he and his wife proclaimed themselves Prince and Princess of Sealand. The Principality has since issued its own passports, currency and stamps.

Other projects include book design for Amsterdam-based publishing house Valiz; website design; a content management system for the Bolivarian Republic of Venezuela in the Netherlands; and brand identity including a poster, flyer and website for *Happening*, a project at the Netherlands Architecture Institute in Rotterdam, curated by Emiliano Gandolfi.

Metahaven also contribute writing to various journals, give lectures all over the world and teach at institutions including Yale University in New Haven, the Academy of Arts in Arnhem and the Sandberg Institute in Amsterdam. Their book, *Uncorporate Identity*, is published by Lars Müller.

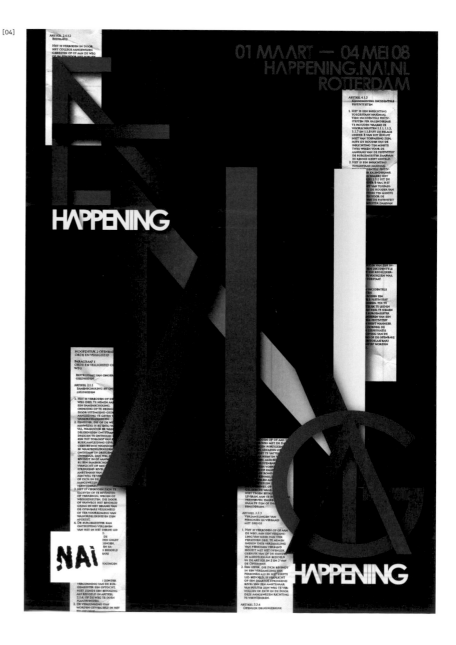

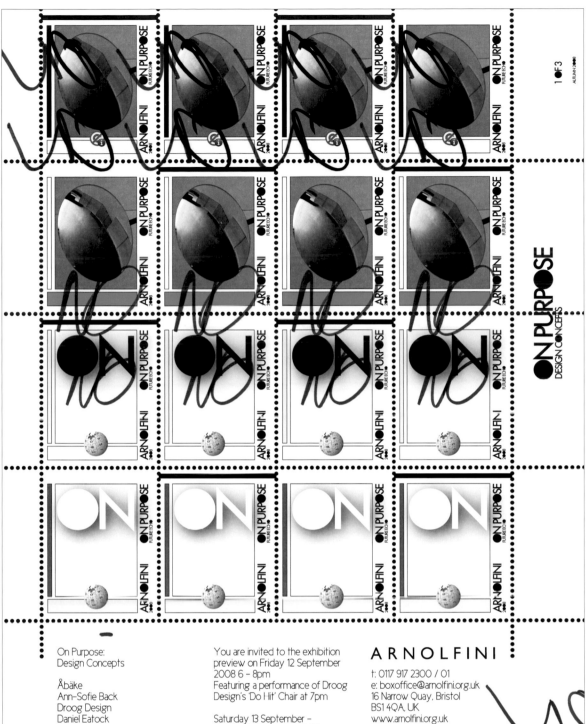

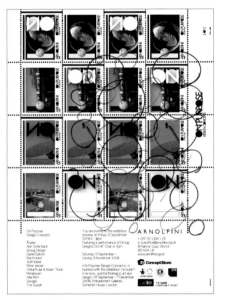

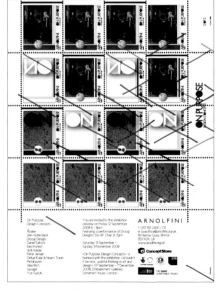

On Purpose:
Design Concepts

Åbäke
Ann-Sofie Back
Droog Design
Daniel Eatock
Electronest
Will Holder
Peter Jensen
Onkar Kular & Noam Toran
Metahaven
Alex Rich
Savage
Yuri Suzuki

You are invited to the exhibition
preview on Friday 12 September
2008 6 – 8pm
Featuring a performance of Droog
Design's 'Do Hit' Chair at 7pm

Saturday 13 September –
Sunday 9 November 2008

∘On Purpose: Design Concepts∘ is
twinned with the exhibition ∘Wouldn't
it be nice... wishful thinking in art and
design∘ (17 September – 7 December
2008), Embankment Galleries,
Somerset House, London

ARNOLFINI

t: 0117 917 2300 / 01
e: boxoffice@arnolfini.org.uk
16 Narrow Quay, Bristol
BS1 4QA, UK
www.arnolfini.org.uk

Concept Store

LOTTERY FUNDED

BRISTOL CITY COUNCIL

375

THE GANE
CHARITABLE TRUST

—

METAHAVEN

Future Echo One, Two, Three

Series of three preview cards for *On Purpose*,
a conceptual design show at Arnolfini
in Fall 2008.

Client Arnolfini, Bristol, UK

BART
DE BAETS

Though born on the Belgium coast, Bart de Baets grew up in Dutch town, Aardenburg. Today based in Amsterdam, he shares a studio with two close friends from where he creates both client projects and his own personal work.

While childhood aspirations included background singing and window dressing, fortunately for the design world, De Baets' high school offered graphic design classes. Of this experience he says: "I liked the restrictions and I liked letters and making them look good. It was a very sexy feeling." He went on to graduate from Gerrit Rietveld Academy in Amsterdam with a degree in graphic design in 2003.

De Baets set up his own studio in 2006, after completing a three-month Artist in Residence programme at Townhouse, a respected gallery in Cairo, Egypt.

Today he works in printed matter, designing invitations, books and posters for cultural clients including Dutch artists such as Melanie Bonajo, Frank Koolen and Heidi Vogels. He also teaches part-time at the Rietveld Academy.

A true author, personal projects are what make De Baets happiest. Currently he creates the wonderfully-titled publication, *Mosquitoes, Elephants, Mountains & Molehills*. Appearing in either poster or magazine format, and published in a small edition by *Onomatopee*, a young publishing duo from the Netherlands, it features "short stories, scribbled-down observations, lists and rumours, and collected or created images." While he says that if it were possible he'd spend all his time working on his own projects, De Baets' dream job would be to make a series of posters. "Something colourful and complex-looking that could be seen all over town, hung in bus-stops and the like."

Inspirations include hard-to-define groups of people, spying, rumours, Claude Closky, Harmony Korine, coincidence, language, old acquaintances, skylines, bridges, zoos, captured moments and talk-shows.

[01]

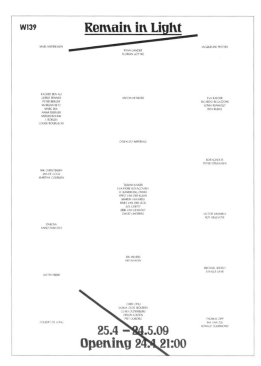

BART DE BAETS

Invitations for an Amsterdam exhibition space. The typographical intervention refers to the upcoming exhibition.

Client W139

[02|03]

INVITATIO 90th

Dear friends,

How are y'all doing? I'm inviting you to my birthday party on Saturday 15 November, starting around 10 o'clock that night. The address hasn't changed, I still live on Camperstraat 59, 1091 AD Amsterdam. Since I'm a little low on dough lately, please skip the presents and just bring some drinks instead. I'll provide you with all the healthy snacks.
Hey! No strangers* this time. The usual crowd already is strange enough. Anyway, please come. I bet it's going to be just great!!!

Your host,

Bart

* You know when you are. More important, you aught to know when you aren't.

This might look like a dress code party. But, actually, it's not. I don't really know why it says GAY in the back.

0652058492

BART DE BAETS

Things To Do Before I Die

Silkscreen poster.

[02] C.A.R.L.

Newsletter for American artist Eric von
Robertson. The newsletter presents his current works that were to be seen in several
galleries or alternative locations in Europe.

Client Eric von Robertson

[03] Mosquitoes, Elephants, Mountains & Molehills

Booklet collecting casually written short stories, observations, lists and rumors, starring
family, friends and lovers, the dead and the
living, the gorgeous and the not so gorgeous.

Publisher Onomatopee
Editors Floor Koomen & Bart De Baets

[04] De Luister van Het Land

Book for Dutch photographer Koen Hauser.
Hauser was asked to create an exhibition in-
spired by the Spaarnestad Newspaper Photo
Archive in Haarlem.

Client Koen Hauser
Editors Koen Hauser & Bart De Baets
Publisher Veenman Publishers

[01]
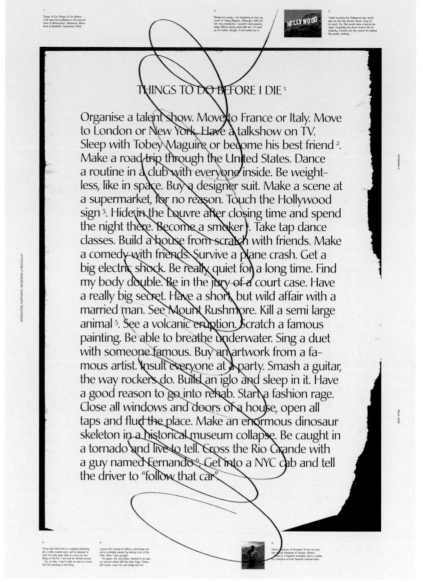

[02]
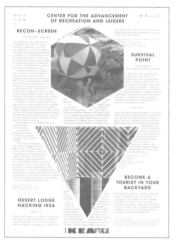

[03]

[04]

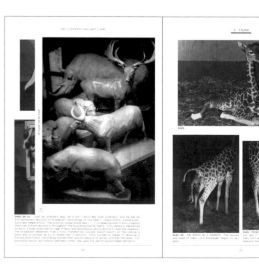

[01]

BART DE BAETS

[01] Visual Music Essay

Assignment brief for the first-year students of the graphic design department of
the Gerrit Rietveld Academy in Amsterdam.

[02] Bart's 28th Birthday Party Invitation

The Assignment #2.
I'd like you to pick something that has your interest, but which is unknown to you to a certain extend. To give a lousy example, if you're the proud owner of a wonderful crown of dreads, choosing Bob Marley wouldn't be much appreciated, let alone surprising, but as I mentioned before, this is a lousy example.

In the end all individual works should be collected and presented as an informative exhibition.
I'll slip you some smaller assign-ments as we go along. Be prepared for those to come. Bring things you like.
Speak up in class and show me visu-als. Showing sketches on paper napkins is no longer allowed from now on.

Tuesday 13 January, 2009
Gerrit Rietveld Academy
Amsterdam

Bart de Baets
www.bartdebaets.nl
bdebaets@gmail.com

Make a Visual Music Essay. Complete, exaggerate, delete. Change around pop history as we know it. Take this chance to create the gig of a lifetime. Think of collectors items, and artifacts. News-paper articles and shocking magazine covers. Outrageous fans, and filthy scandals, platinum records, concert post-ers, Pop-charts, phenomenal concerts, surprising come-backs, break-throughs, and devastating break-ups.

[02]

BART DE BAETS
CAMPERSTRAAT 59
06-52058492

10.11.2007.   *28

**BIRTHDAY*PARTY AT
MY PLACE, STARTING
ROUND 21.00. COME BY AND
ENJOY THE LOVELY EXTRAS:**
Champagne Showers, Excellent Bare-back Opportunities, Zjeneuver Kotje*, Free Cocaine on the Roof Terrace, *more than 30 different flavours* Marc Jacobs Goodie-bag, Hot Lap-dances by Lil' Kim, Bullfighting, Mon-ster Make-Overs by a Professional Team, World Cup on Big TV Screen, Garbage Recycling Workshops, Guided Tours, Private Karaoke Booth, Tattoo & Piercing Studio, Free Wireless Internet, Relax Booth with Lego, Live Contact with Aliens, Ibiza DJ line up, Chinese Dragons, Lots of Naked Stuff, Absolute Overdose Lounge Hall, Free Interior Decorating Tips & Fireworks, Your Host, BdB

BRING DRINKS, ALWAYS BRING DRINKS!!

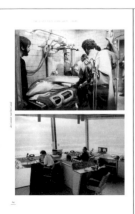

[01]

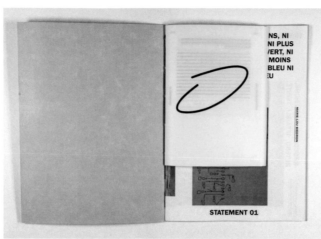
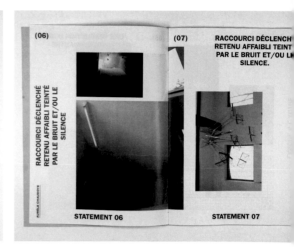

[02]

New York City, USA
181 North 11th Street, Suite 406, Brooklyn, New York 11211
—Office:
+1 646 277 7117
—Fax:
+1 718 290 9141

Paris, France
14 Avenue Claude Vellefaux, Paris, France 75010
—Office:
+33 1 42031039

AREA 17

Adam
Arnaud
David

Dominique
George
Kemp

Mubs
Jordan
Fabienne

Brice Domingues ©

—
BRICE DOMINGUES

[01] Workshop CAC Parc Saint Léger

The Book is the result of a workshop with the École des Beaux Arts de Dijon and Esaab Nevers on the work of Lawrence Wiener.

Clients École des Beaux Arts de Dijon, Esaab Nevers

[02] Area17

Client Area17 / Arnaud Mercier

[03] Association de Designeurs

Identity for *Association de Designeurs*.

Client Association de Designeurs

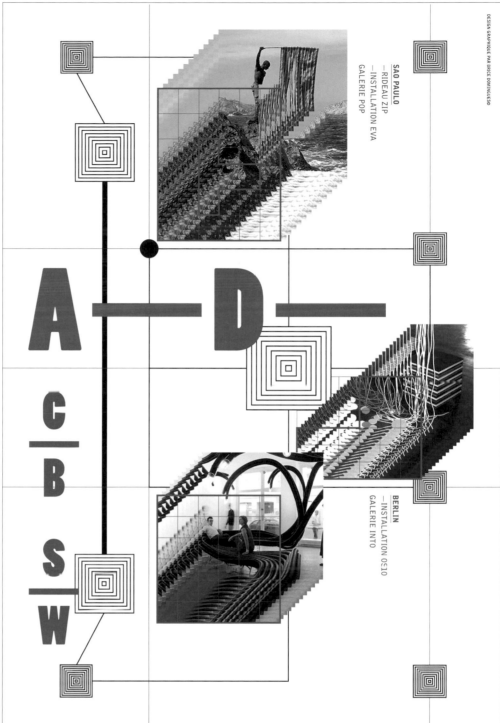

DESIGN GRAPHIQUE PAR BRICE DOMINGUES9

SAO PAULO
—RIDEAU ZIP
—INSTALLATION EVA
GALERIE POP

BERLIN
—INSTALLATION 0S10
GALERIE INTO

ASSOCIATION DE DESIGNEURS

7 RUE FORTIA 13001 MARSEILLE FRANCE

—CHRISTOPHE BAILLEUX
—SEBASTIEN WIERINCK

WWW.ASSODESIGNEURS.COM

DESIGN L.N BOUL
PHOTO D.BOSCHI

DESIGN M.PEYRE

DESIGN S.WIERINCK
PHOTO F.SEEHAUSEN

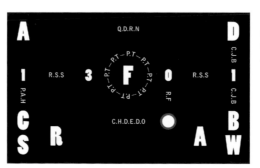

A—D—

ASSOCIATION DE DESIGNEURS
7 RUE FORTIA
13001 MARSEILLE
FRANCE
WWW.ASSODESIGNEURS.COM

CHRISTOPHE BAILLEUX
+33 (0)6 79 18 15 66
CB@ASSODESIGNEURS.COM

SEBASTIEN WIERINCK
+33 (0)6 32 49 31 12
SW@ASSODESIGNEURS.COM

BRICE DOMINGUES
P. 30–33

French designer Brice Domingues is self-taught. Born in Marseilles in 1979, Domingues graduated with a bachelor's degree in Biology from the Université de Provence in his hometown in 2000, and went on to receive his masters degree in Cinema from the Université de La Garde in Toulon in 2004. Domingues' interest in design did not come as an epiphany but rather a gradual awakening, inspired first by Booth-Clibborn's book *Specials* (2001), which he explains, "was an excellent starting point to 'decomplexify' the rules and uses of graphic design."

Spurred on by his selection for the Biennial of Young Artists from Europe and the Mediterranean, held in Naples in 2005, Domingues took the leap and launched his graphic design career immediately afterwards.

Still based in Marseilles, Domingues enjoys commissions for cultural clients including the Espace Culture Marseille, the Contemporary Art Centre in Istres, designer Sébastien Wierinck, *Useless* magazine, and the School of Fine Arts in Toulouse. Though he tends to work alone, Domingues sometimes collaborates on projects with fellow designers Catherine Guiral and Alain Delluc under the name of *officeabc*.

He is inspired by: "Béla Tarr and his films, the vernacular, Robert Johnson's legend, the recent book by Georges Didi-Huberman *Quand les images prennent position*, and anything that questions the role of design and art and their processes."

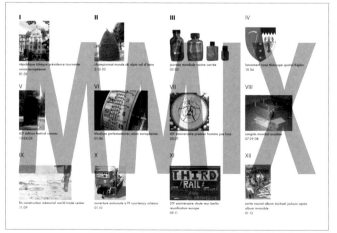

BRICE DOMINGUES, ALAIN DELLUC & ADRIAAN MELLEGERS

[01, 04] Frac

Poster Researching New Identity for Frac Centre.

Client Frac Centre

BRICE DOMINGUES & OFFICEABC

[02] New Year Card 2009

Client Esba Toulouse

BRICE DOMINGUES

[03] Anthropolis Poster

Client Anthropolis

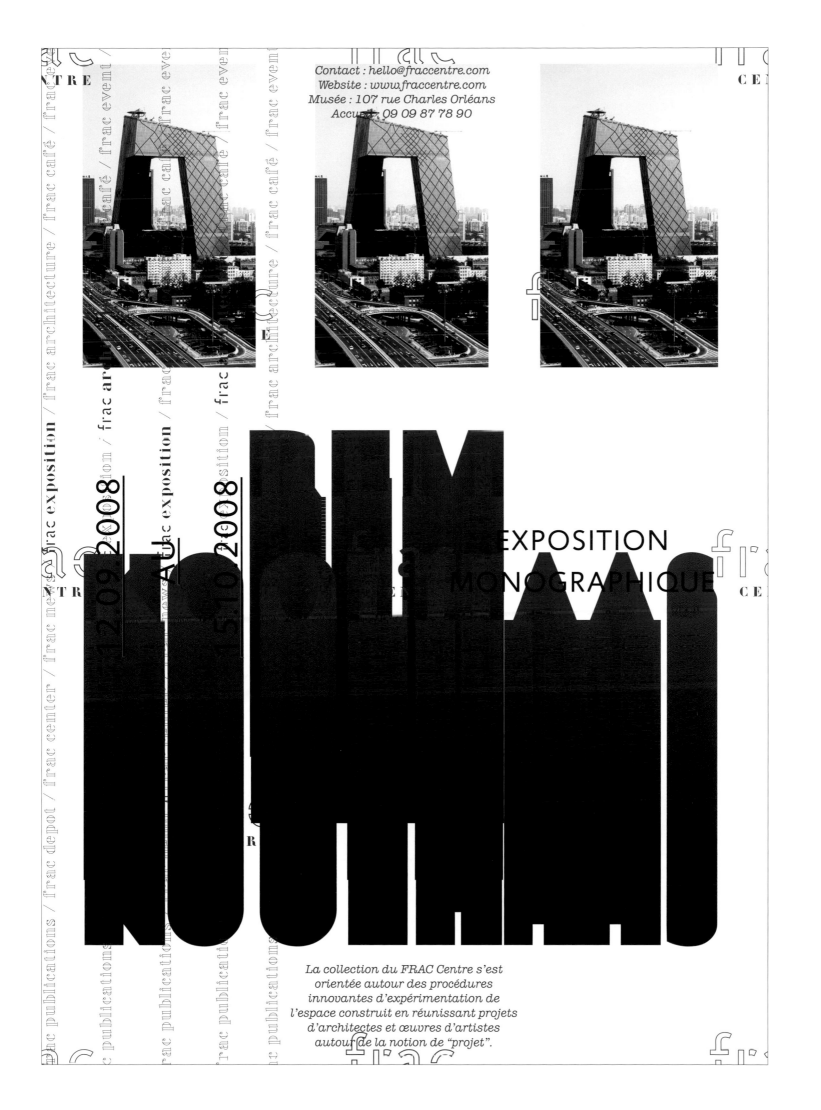

Contact : hello@fraccentre.com
Website : www.fraccentre.com
Musée : 107 rue Charles Orléans
Accueil : 09 09 87 78 90

12.09.2008

15.10.2008

EXPOSITION
MONOGRAPHIQUE

REM
KOOLHAAS

La collection du FRAC Centre s'est
orientée autour des procédures
innovantes d'expérimentation de
l'espace construit en réunissant projets
d'architectes et œuvres d'artistes
autour de la notion de "projet".

TYPO-GRAPHY

Typography involves both the creation of text fonts itself and the application of type in the context of an overall typographic layout. Between the poles of these two typographic activities, the creation of a sufficiently strong visual appeal and the avoidance of overly streamlined forms are of critical importance. However, neither of these two elements alone is a guarantee for good legibility. Broadly speaking, the typographic design of posters, books or the editorial layout of newspapers and magazines can be categorised into two extremes, with no identifiable middle ground being occupied between them. Alongside the prevailing trend towards austere objectivity which rejects ornamental effects and always favours sober clarity over superfluous exuberance, there is also an observable movement towards experimentation, deconstruction, disruption and destruction. Neo-conservative works employ standard sans serif fonts such as Futura, Typewriter, Univers or Helvetica in unusual contexts, thus breaking from the connotations associated with these fonts, and elsewhere, stroke and signmaker fonts are beginning to be used again more frequently. Agencies such as vier5 started using significant disruptions, omissions and emphases very early on, and more designers than ever are now employing extreme stylistic methods in the design of their fonts. Experimental fonts are being distorted into abstract forms to such an extent that they are barely recognisable or legible. Alongside this, tactile elements also continue to be fashionable, with typographers developing playful three-dimensional letter models which are then used as a basis for deriving other fonts later on. The design of original letters and fonts also draws upon the specific qualities of hand-lettering and calligraphy.

A COLLECTIVE MEMORY.
TYPEFACE FOR THE 5TH BERLIN BIENNIAL FOR CONTEMPORARY ART 2008.

ject of the 5th Berlin
for Contemporary Art
s all the visual
ication of the event.
diums include billboards,
flyers, postcards,
dmission tickets and
on guides.

loped a specific
e for the visual
ication of the event.
iculaity of this typeface
contains images
tter "B" and in the figure
for Berlin and Biennial,
he 5th edition.

mages represent places
ects of Berlin. The objects
om the "Museum der
(Museum of Things),
m which has collected
gn objects that made
history in Germany in the
tury.

tures of the places have
ken nowadays. The
n of these places is
ve: they can be famous
of Berlin, as well as
n places. They are
ts of a possible walk
Berlin.

mages of objects and
ntegrated in the letter,
a possible collective
y of the city.
al alphabet, which brings
and its history to light,
acts the topic and the
he Biennial:
hings
Shadow".

OUTSKIRTS OF BERLIN

SILO BUILDING

DURING DEMOLITION
UNTER DEN LINDEN, BERLIN MITTE

PALACE OF THE REPUBLIC

"PLATTENBAU"

ADAM OPEL HAUS

HOTEL RITZ-CARLTON

BLACK & YELLOW ALARM-CLOCK

2

3

A Group Show :

Wednesday **10** June – Friday **12** June 2009
20.30h : Theater Basel Grosse Bühne
Tickets : www.theater-basel.ch
Organised by :
Art Basel Fondation Beyeler Theater Basel

I L

TEM 7
PO 6 OS
ZINO

DEL

Doug Aitken
Matthew Barney
& Jonathan Bepler
Tacita Dean
Thomas Demand
Trisha Donnelly
Olafur Eliasson
Peter Fischli / David Weiss
Liam Gillick
Dominique
Gonzalez-Foerster
Douglas Gordon
Carsten Höller
Pierre Huyghe
Koo Jeong-A
Philippe Parreno
Anri Sala
Tino Sehgal
Rirkrit Tiravanija
& Arto Lindsay

What
if an
exhibition
was not about occupying space
but about occupying time?

Curated by :
Hans Ulrich Obrist
Philippe Parreno

Directed by :
Hans Ulrich Obrist
Philippe Parreno
Anri Sala
Rirkrit Tiravanija

Originally commissioned by
Manchester International Festival
Théâtre du Châtelet Paris

TYPOGRAPHY CABINET

The Type Gazette – Issue N°1, May 2009

Review for typography.

Credit: Edited and designed
by Ludovic Balland —Typography Cabinet.

[01]

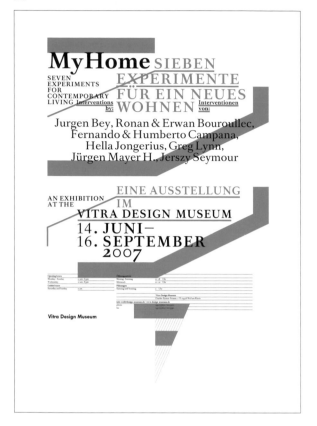

LUDOVIC BALLAND
TYPOGRAPHY CABINET

[01]   My Home

Poster for an exhibition at the Vitra Design
Museum, which presented seven experiments
for contemporary living.

Client Vitra AG, Birsfelden

[02]   Building Vitra: New Projects

Poster for an exhibition organised by Vitra.

Client Vitra AG, Birsfelden

[03]   5th Berlin Biennial for Contemporary Art
Lecture at the Museum of Modern Art in Warsaw

Poster for the lecture of Adam Szymczyk and
Elena Filipovic at the Museum of Modern Art
in Warsaw, related to the 5th Berlin Biennial
for Contemporary Art.

Client Museum of Modern Art, Warsaw

[02]

ISR-Spazio Culturale Svizzero
di Venezia
Campo Sant'Agnese, Dorsoduro 810

September 12–30, 2008
daily :
10:00–
18:00

Building Vitra :
New
Projects
by
Herzog & de Meuron
SANAA
Alejandro Aravena

An exhibition on the development of the Vitra Site
organized by Vitra Design Foundation
in collaboration with ISR-Spazio Culturale Svizzero di Venezia

photos by Olivo Barbieri,
Gabriele Basilico,
Giovanni Chiaramonte,
Paola De Pietri

September 12, 2008
at 11:00 Accademia di Belle Arti
di Venezia :
Aula Magna,
Ex Ospedale degli Incurabili,
Zattere, Dorsoduro 423
Jacques Herzog
Alejandro Aravena

A conference organized by
Vitra Design Foundation
in collaboration with
Accademia di Belle Arti di Venezia

September 12–November 30, 2008
Campo Sant'Agnese Dorsoduro, Venezia
"Behind my back Vitra Headquarters by
F.O. Gehry" by Vincenzo Casali with the
support of Vitra Design Foundation,
Comune di Venezia Galleria Contemporaneo
An outdoor installation

GOETHE
INSTITUT
WARSZAWA
MUZEUM
SZTUKI
NOWOCZESNEJ
W WARSZAWIE

ZAPRASZAJĄ NA
PREZENTACJĘ PIĄTEGO

BERLIN
BIENNALE

PROGRAM WYSTAWY I ARTYSTÓW
BIORĄCYCH W NIEJ UDZIAŁ PRZEDSTAWIĄ
KURATORZY BIENNALE:
ADAM SZYMCZYK
I
ELENA FILIPOVIC

16.02.2008
GODZINA 18.00

Muzeum Sztuki Nowoczesnej w Warszawie
ulica Pańska 3
wejście od strony hotelu Intercontinental
www.artmuseum.pl
www.goethe.de/warschau
www.berlinbiennale.info

Design: Ludovic Balland, Typography Office Basel

GOETHE-INSTITUT
WARSCHAU

left right up down under over around in between in front behind in out and back again.

Julian Bittiner
Stina Carlberg
Tomáš Celizna
Daniel Harding
Dawn Joseph
Jin-Yeoul Jung

Emily Larned
Lan Lan Liu
Thomas Manning
Ken Meier
Min Oh
Bethany Powell

Nicholas Rock
Stewart Smith
Fan Wu
David Yun
Roxane Zargham

MFA Graphic Design
Thesis Exhibition
May 10–14, 2008
Opening May 10, 7 pm
Yale School of Art
Green Hall Gallery

An installation by 17 graduate graphic design students at the Yale School of Art.   art.yale.edu/gdshow

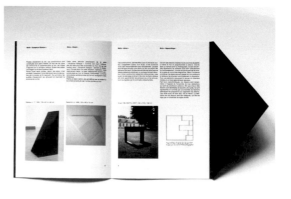

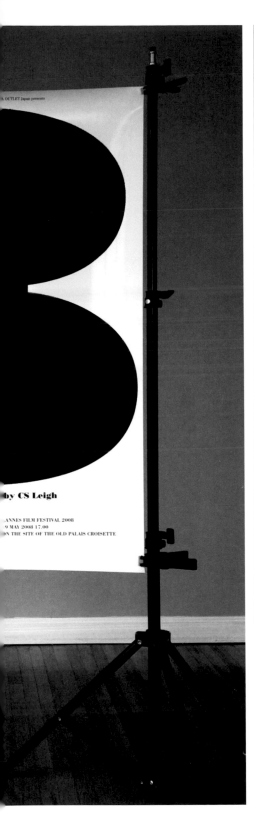

JULIAN BITTINER

[01, 04] Left Right Up Down

Invitation poster announcing the 2008
Yale MFA Graphic Design Thesis Exhibition
at the Yale School of Art.

Client / Publisher Yale School of Art

[05] Process Picture

Custom typeface designed for the Yale
Graphic Design MFA Thesis Exhibition 2008.

Client Yale School of Art

XAVIER ENCINAS

[02] Cannes 6808

Poster for CS Leigh's film performance
at the 2008 Cannes Film Festival

Client CS Leigh

[06] Deux au Carré

Poster for Deux au Carré exhibition with artists Koyo Hara and Jena-Gabriel Coignet.

Client Carré St Anne

RAF VANCAMPENHOUDT &
JORIS VAN AKEN

[03] Le Locataire

Movie poster design for *The Tenant* by Roman Polanski. One out of a series of posters
designed for Wim Lambrecht's Movie Nights
at Sint-Lucas Visual Arts, Ghent.

Client Wim Lambrecht, Ghent, Belgium

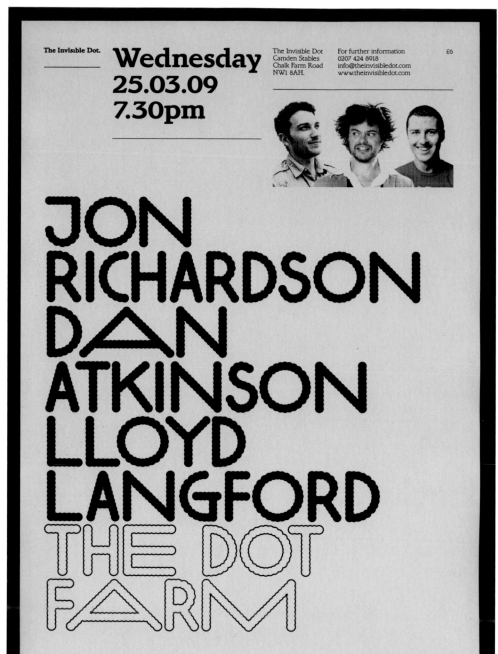

The Invisible Dot.

Wednesday
25.03.09
7.30pm

The Invisible Dot
Camden Stables
Chalk Farm Road
NW1 8AH.

For further information
0207 424 8918
info@theinvisibledot.com
www.theinvisibledot.com

£6

JON
RICHARDSON
DAN
ATKINSON
LLOYD
LANGFORD
THE DOT
FARM

JULIA

The Invisible Dot Identity

Identity for a comedy production company recently established in North London. Posters created using injekt Risograph printer.

Client The Invisible Dot Ltd

—
VELINA STOYKOVA

[01] The Shining

Poster for the Stanley Kubrick movie
The Shining.

Client Werkplaats Typografie

—
SANDRA KASSENAAR

[02] *Faugh a Ballaugh / Cowabunga*

Silkcreen poster with 6 different colours.

Client Project in collaboration with bookshop split,
Fountain in Auckland, New Zealand

[01|02]

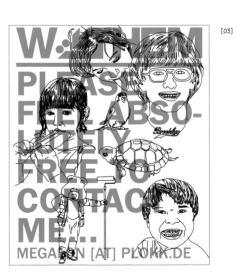

[03]

[04]

—
NA KIM

[01] Starting from Zero

Poster and booklet for an exhibition.

Client Werkplaats Typografie (NL),
Zero One Design Center (KR)

—
KONST & TEKNIK

[02] Klubb:Europa

Identity for Klubb:Europa, a club tour
traveling through Sweden with DJs from
six different European countries, initiated
by the Goethe-Institut and the German
Embassy in Stockholm.

Client / Publisher Goethe Institute/ The German Embassy, Sweden

—
W//:THEM
Floyd Schulze

[03] W//:THEM.family

Self-promotional poster.

—
SÉRGIO ALVES

[04] Bom Tĩa

Poster and type design.

Client Bom Dia Project

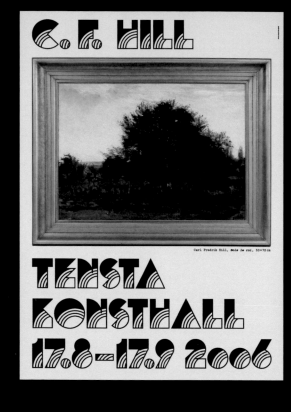
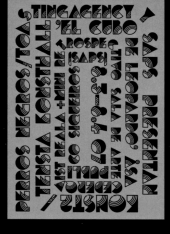

JONAS WILLIAMSSON

[01] Tensta Konsthall

Identity commissioned by Tensta Konsthall. Originally developed in collaboration with Swedish artist Karl Holmqvist.

Client / Publisher / Editor Tensta Konsthall

TOBIAS RÖTTGER

[02] Shopi

Client Shopi

[03] MRI vs. UES

Record-Cover

Client MRI
Publisher RS

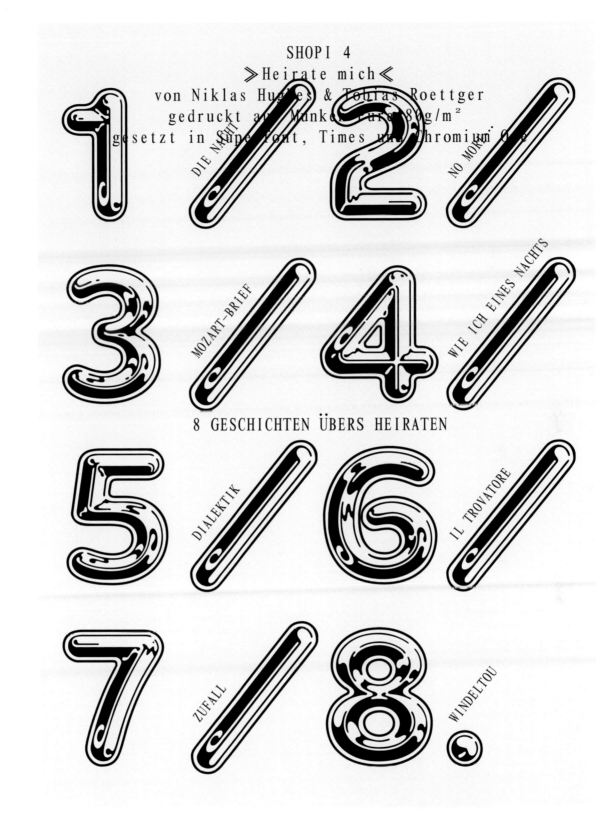

SHOP I 4
≫Heirate mich≪
von Niklas Hughes & Tobias Roettger
gedruckt auf Munken Pure 80g/m²
gesetzt in Super Font, Times und Chromium One

DIE NACHT / NO MORE /
MOZART-BRIEF / WIE ICH EINES NACHTS /

8 GESCHICHTEN ÜBERS HEIRATEN

DIALEKTIK / IL TROVATORE /
ZUFALL / WINDELTOU

[01]

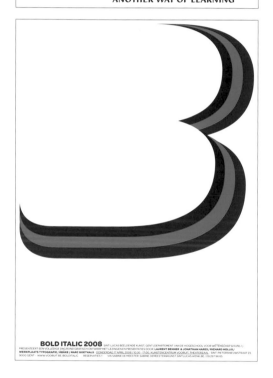

[04]

[03]

**RAF VANCAMPENHOUDT &
JORIS VAN AKEN**

[01] Drawing, Another Way of Learning

Poster design for a symposium about drawing at Sint-Lucas Visual Arts, Ghent.

Client Ans Nys, Ghent, Belgium

RAF VANCAMPENHOUDT

[02] Bold Italic 2008

Poster design for the Bold Italic 2008 event, an annual symposium about graphic design and typography organized by Michaël Bussaer of Sint-Lucas Visual Arts, Ghent.

Client Michaël Bussaer / Vooruit

[03] The Best of Italo Disco

Poster as part of a master's thesis about Italo disco, an electronic music phenomenon which finds its origins in Italy in the early eighties.

VOIDWRECK
Karl Nawrot & Jaan Evart

[04] Abstraktsioonide Öö / The Night of Abstractions Volume 3

Poster for an Estonian experimental electronic music night.

Client Festival Hea Uus Heli
Credits Mark typeface by Karl Nawrot / Poster design by Jaan Evart

VOIDWRECK
Karl Nawrot, Jaan Evart & Walter Warton

[05] Kumu Öö / Kumu Night

Poster for a music festival in the Modern Art Museum of Tallinn.

Client Festival Hea Uus Heli

HANSAPANK ESITLEB

KUMU

ooo

PLANNINGTOROCK (de)
MUGISON (is)
SUSANNA (no)

THE ORB (uk)

20 REEDEL JUUNIL

plaate esitlevad
STELLA
KÖÖK
UMA (A.Saks & R.Jürjendal)
CLOUDSPEAK
MAIKAMEIKERS

THEY CAME FROM THE
STARS I SAW THEM (uk)
HAUSCHKA (de)
FUSED MARC (lt)
ES + Sami Sänpäkkilä
lühifilmid

WWW.HUH.EE

WWW.FBI.EE

MARCO MÜLLER

[01] Good for pushing down a piano pedal

Art exhibition, live lithography printing and lunch of André Wilhelms artist book *Peanutsfactory*.

Client André Wilhelm
Editor Graphische Anstalt
J. E. Wolfensberger AG, Zürich
Credits Handwriting by Pat Squires, London

NODE BERLIN OSLO

[02] Happy Days Sound Festival

Poster, banners and brochure working with the beauty of traditional calligraphy contrasted with curses like *helvete* (hell) and *faen* (goddamn).

Client Ny Musikk (Norwegian section of the International Society for Contemporary Music)
Credits Calligraphy by Bård Ydén

---

[03] JULIAN BITTINER

Dawdle & Gape

Poster and exhibition packaging for the travelling exhibition Dawdle & Gape: Yale Graphic Design Thesis Books 2008.

Client Yale School of Art
Editor Julian Bittiner, Sheila Levrant de Bretteville
Publisher Yale School of Art

KATJA GRETZINGER & GREGOR HUBER

[04] Fabrikzeitung

Newspaper for a concert hall.

Client Rote Fabrik Zürich

[01]

PEANUTSFACTORY
26. Januar 2007, 15.–21.00 Uhr
—
die Peanutsfactory stellt sich vor:
– Buchprojekt
– Künstler André Wilhelm
  im Steindruckatelier
– Werkgruppe

Besuchen Sie uns ganztags
bei der Arbeit mit André Wilhelm.
Anmeldung bitte an:
steindruck@wolfensberger-ag.ch

Graphische Anstalt
J. E. Wolfensberger AG
Steindruckerei
Eglistrasse 8
8004 Zürich

Telefon: 044 285 78 78
www.wolfensberger-ag.ch

GOOD FOR PUSHING DOWN A PIANO PEDAL

[02]

Daw-dle & Gape

17*

Designer: Stewart Smith
Title: Boothrop
Dimensions: variable
Number of pages: variable
Binding: variable

Excerpt
While the term 'hacker' may carry negative connotations and seem confined to computer programming, Stewart is interested in the more general (and positive) definition. One who produces clever conceptual twists in systems. The Jargon File also notes that a hack can be "a brilliant take where neatness is correlated with cleverness, harmlessness, and surprise value."

"This book is not featured as a standalone object. Rather, it comprises to individual documents which reside discreetly – like a virus – inside the other thesis books.

Yale Graphic Design Thesis Books 2008

[03]

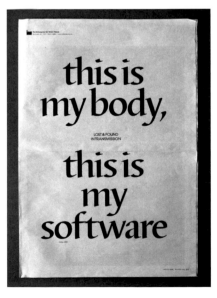

[04]

KARL NAWROT

Karl Nawrot is a French designer who lives and works in Amsterdam, the Netherlands. Born in 1976 in Villeurbanne, France, Nawrot graduated with a master's degree in illustration from Emile Cohl, Lyon in 1998. Ten years later, in 2008, he graduated with a second master's degree in Graphic Design at the Werkplaats Typografie in Arnhem, the Netherlands.

While Nawrot set up his own studio in Amsterdam in 2009, he also teaches at the Gerrit Rietveld Academy and occasionally works on self-initiated projects with designer Walter Warton under the name of Void Wreck. Personal clients to date have included: the Dutch Art Institute in Enschede, Berlin-based record label EN/OF Records, Lüttgenmeijer gallery, also in Berlin, MUSAC (Museum of Contemporary Art) in Castilla y León, Spain and *The New York Times*.

When Nawrot moved to the Netherlands from France, he brought with him just five books. A *Letraset®* catalog (1980), a French version of *Nekojiru Udon* 3 by Nekojiru (Imho, 2006), *Typography* by Emil Ruder (Niggli, 1967), *The Enshedé Catalog of Typographic Borders & Ornaments* (Dover, 1986) and a bilingual (English/French) short story, *The Monkey* by Stephen King (Pocket, 2005). These, he says, are his main inspiration.

Aside from these five titles, Nawrot explains that many of his ideas come from an eight-year period before he moved to the Netherlands during which he filled sketchbooks with "daily drawings, unfinished stories and hand-drawn typefaces". "Most of my work today is based on these ideas," he continues, "I don't think I have changed so much since this period, my ideas have just become clearer. What you see in my work today, objects or typefaces, is the result of some of these untold stories".

[01]

LÜTTGENMEIJER
SCHILLINGSTRAßE 31
10179 BERLIN
MAIL@LUETTGENMEIJER.COM
T.+49 (0)30 2804 5805

OPENING
15/03/08, 19:00–21:00
OPEN
TUESDAY–SATURDAY
12:00–18:00

CHRIS EVANS

WHAT'S THE POINT OF REVOLUTION WITHOUT COPULATION, COPULATION COPULATION?

15/03– 26/04/08

[02]

LÜTTGENMEIJER
SCHILLINGSTRAßE 31
10179 BERLIN
MAIL@LUETTGENMEIJER.COM
T.+49 (0)30 2804 5805

OPENING
14/02/09, 19:00–21:00
OPEN
TUESDAY–SATURDAY
12:00–18:00

LÜTTGENMEIJER
SCHILLINGSTRAßE 31
10179 BERLIN
MAIL@LUETTGENMEIJER.COM
T.+49 (0)30 2804 5805

OPENING
10/10/08, 19:00–21:00
OPEN
TUESDAY–SATURDAY
12:00–18:00

MATTHEW SMITH

AS GREY AS THOSE BENDS

14/02– 14/03/09

MATT CONNORS

HOMONYMS

10/10– 08/11/08

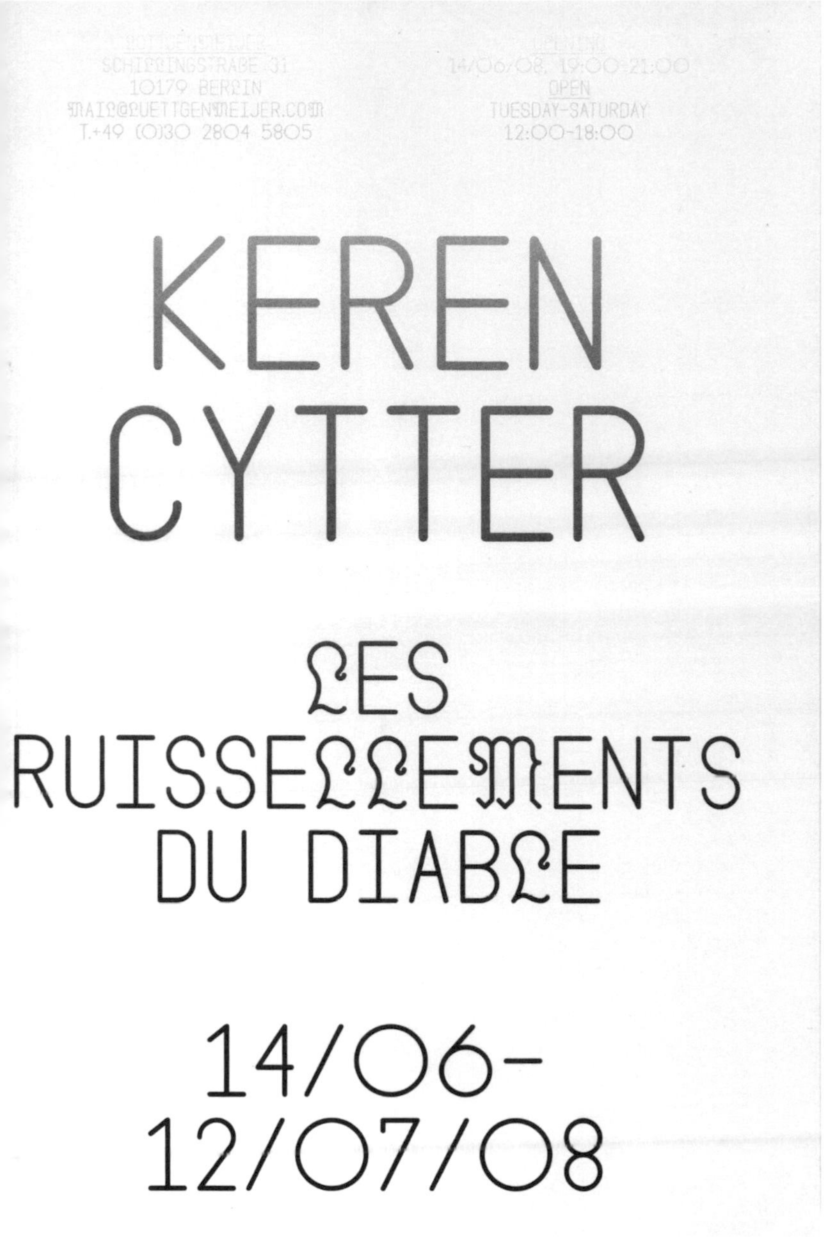

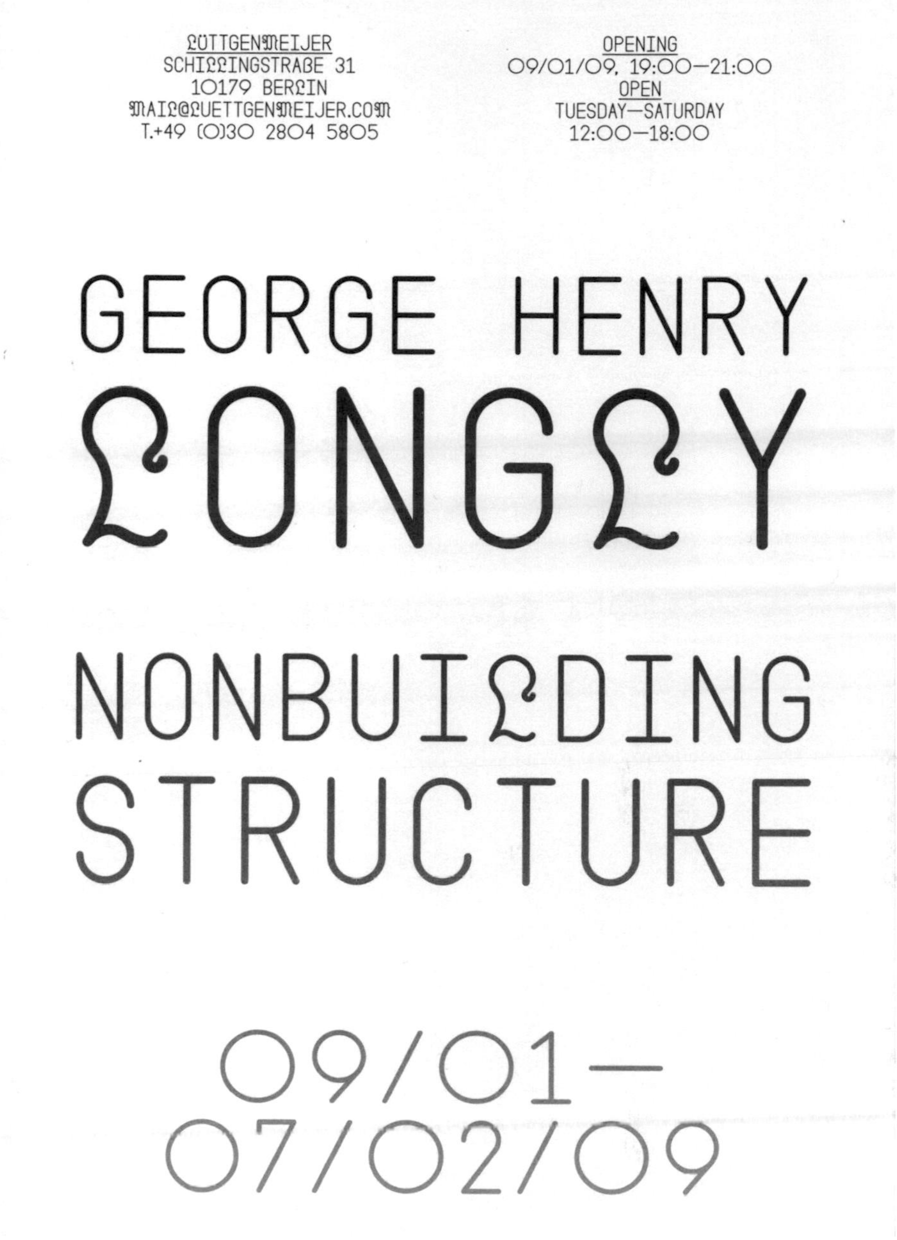

ℒÜTTGENℳEIJER
SCHIℒℒINGSTRAßE 31
1O179 BERℒIN
ℳAIℒ@ℒUETTGENℳEIJER.COℳ
T.+49 (O)3O 28O4 58O5

OPENING
O9/O1/O9, 19:OO—21:OO
OPEN
TUESDAY—SATURDAY
12:OO—18:OO

KEREN CYTTER

ℒES RUISSEℒℒEℳENTS DU DIABℒE

14/O6— 12/O7/O8

GEORGE HENRY ℒONGℒY

NONBUIℒDING STRUCTURE

O9/O1— O7/O2/O9

ℒÜTTGENℳEIJER
SCHIℒℒINGSTRAßE 31
1O179 BERℒIN
ℳAIℒ@ℒUETTGENℳEIJER.COℳ
T.+49 (O)3O 28O4 58O5

OPENING
O2/O5/O8, 18:OO—21:OO
OPEN
TUESDAY—SATURDAY
12:OO—18:OO

JASON DODGE

O2/O5— O7/O6/O8

—
VOIDWRECK
Karl Nawrot

[01] Lüttgenmeijer 11 Invitations 11 Paper Heads

The identity for the Berlin art gallery Lüttgenmeijer is a custom drawn typeface. Only
the letters L and M are different from the
whole set. The flyer is printed on A4 and used
as letter head.

Client Lüttgenmeijer

[02] Exercise I

Series of typefaces drawn with self-made or
founded tools.

The Festival to Plead for Skills presents:

Date _____

Place _____

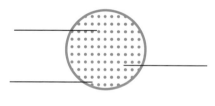

The future of the book seems to point more and more towards digital media. This will surely affect the way we design content, and the linearity of a bound book will soon to be challenged by the interactivity of electronic devices. Join this open talk to discuss what the true impact of this change will be.

For more information please visit www.house-hold.org

The Festival to Plead for Skills presents:

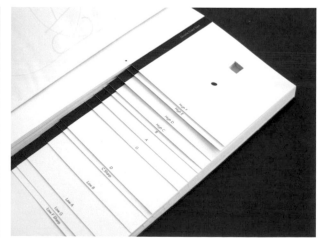

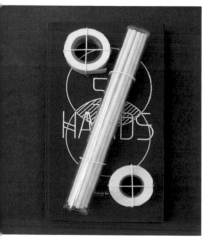

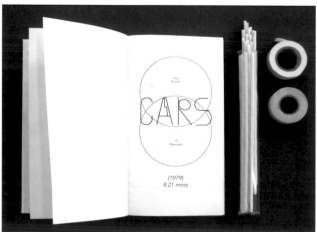

HOUSEHOLD

[01] Future of the Book –
The Festival to Plead for Skills

The future of the book seems to point more and more towards digital media. Posters to advertise a series of workshops discussing what the true impact of this change will be.

[02] 50 Hands – The Festival to Plead for Skills

Can you make an orchestra in a day? Poster for a collaborative musical workshop with 25 people.

[03] T.O.D

Back side of type specimen poster for T.O.D.

[04] 50 Hands – a Household Orchestra

Portable music kit in book form for a one-day Orchestra. The book was produced for the exhibition *The cover of a book is the beginning of a journey* at Arnolfini, Bristol.

Client Arnolfini gallery, Bristol, UK
Credits Collaboration with Yuri Suzuki

HUBERTUS

[05–06] Creative Wednesday

Poster, flyer and booklet.

Client Creative Wednesday Zurich

[05]

[06]

KOEHORST IN 'T VELD

The Great Indoors Awards

Identity for International Design Award.

Client The Great Indoors Awards

GUILLAUME MOJON
[from left to right]

*Georg Gatsas & Lizzi Bougatsos
at Zoo Art Fair, London*

*Daniel Gustav Cramer & Haris Epaminonda
at Nada Art Fair, Miami 2008*

X m3 Galerieraum (Leer)

Eva

Life is Fragile

Empty Centres

Invite / newsletter system develop for exhibitions and events happening in parallel to the BolteLang's gallery program.

Client BolteLang

TOMAS CELIZNA & DANIEL HARDING

[01]   Gisela Noack's Bookbinding Workshops

Poster made of four perforated and perfectly bound stacks of paper, where each set of 4 tiled sheets has different typeface and/or colour. Passers-by were invited to remove individual sheets.

[02]   Daniël van der Velden

Poster for Daniël's first visit as a critic in the graphic design program at Yale. The poster re-appropriates his work for Metahaven, the *Sealand Identity Project* in particular, and also references Daniël's use of re-appropriation in his own work.

[01]

[02]

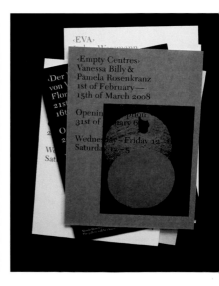

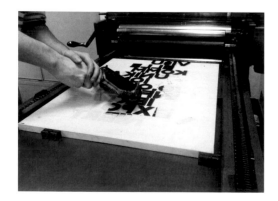

**DENNY BACKHAUS
& PER TÖRNBERG**

[01]   Rietveld Eindexamen Party 2007

Posters for the final exam party of Gerrit
Rietveld Academy which took place in two
clubs at the same time. The posters can be
hung as a whole, or cut in the middle and
recomposed in order to communicate the
information about the two clubs.

Client Gerrit Rietveld Academie
Credits Randoom Typeface by Philippe Egger

STUDIO SPORT
Martin Stoecklin & Andrea Koch

[02]   Informiert / Exponiert

Poster for an information event at the visual
communications department of the Zurich
University of Arts.

Client / Publisher Visual communications department of
the Zurich University of Arts, ZHdK
Editors Andrea Koch, Martin Stoecklin,
Rudolf Barmettler
Credits Rudolf Barmettler for supervision and cri-
tique, Typewriter-typeface Lacrima by
Alexander Meyer

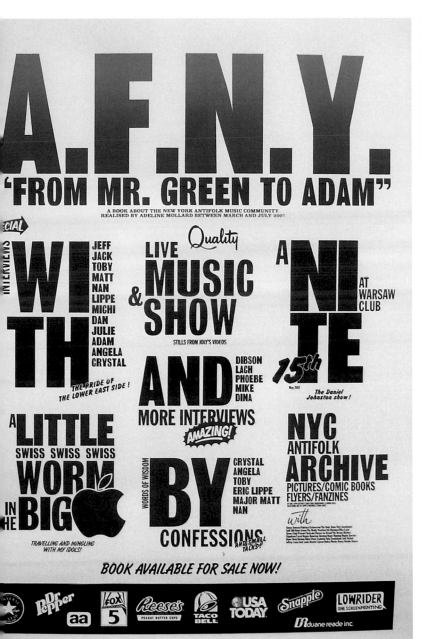

FAGETA
Adeline Mollard

A.F.N.Y

Poster announcing the book *From Mr. Green
to Adam* about the New York antifolk
music community.

I'M STRAIGHT,
I'M GAY,
I'M SO L.A.

STRAIGHT
STRAIGHT
STRAIGHT

STRAIGHT
STRAIGHT
STRAIGHT
STRAIGHT
STRAIGHT
STRAIGHT
STRAIGHT
STRAIGHT
STRAIGHT

BABES
BABES
BABES
BABES
BABES
BABES
BABES
BABES
BABES
BABES

STRAIGHT BABES

A TYPEFACE

ZUCKER UND PFEFFER
Denny Backhaus

[01]   Straight Babes Typeface

GUILLAUME MOJON

[02]   STOYKOVA

Poster for the graduation of Velina Stoykova
from the Werkplaats Typografie in 2008.
Client David Bennewith for
the Werkplaats Typografie

[03]   Specimen Kleber

Specimen made to present the font *Kleber*.
On each page of the book a different character is printed.

[05]   Martin Majoor: Helvetica was a Mistake

Poster made for the lecture 'Helvetica was a
Mistake' by Martin Majoor at the Werkplaats
Typografie in 2006.
Client Werkplaats Typografie

[06]   The Corridor – Forms of Inquiry:
The Architecture of Critical Graphic Design

Identity for The Corridor, BolteLang's project
space for new commissions, site-specific installations and exhibitions. It is a space with
restricted dimensions, related to the main
gallery only geographically and therefore
completely open to experimentation.
Client BolteLang

JUNG UND WENIG
Christopher Jung & Tobias Wenig

[04]   Die Akzidenz Grotesk

Poster series and specimen for the Museum
of the Printing Arts, Leipzig.

---

[02]

STOYKOVA
ASTOYKOV
VASTOYKO
OVASTOYK
KOVASTOY
YKOVASTO
OYKOVAST
TOYKOVAS
STOYKOVA

Stoykova's Graduation – Werkplaats Typografie – 2008
Poster: Guillaume Mojon

[03]

specimen KLEBER: zauothen

AKZIDENZ GROTESK   H. BERTHOLD AG 1896

MUSEUM FÜR DRUCKKUNST
NONNENSTR. 38
04229 LEIPZIG

Museum

F. DRUCK 1234
KUNST 04229
The ABCleipzig
DEFGHIijklmnopq
JKLMNOstuvwxyz
PQRSTU+
VWXYZ
schrift AkzidenzGr
otesk.

LIGHT *LIGHTITALIC* NORMAL *ITALIC* **MEDIUM** *MEDIUMITALIC* **BOLD** ***BOLDITALIC*** **BLACK**

24 pt   24pt

ÖFFNUNGSZEITEN:
MONTAG – FREITAG
10:00 – 17:00 H
SAMS. GESCHLOSSEN
SONNTAG
11:00 – 17:00 H

WWW.DRUCKKUNST-MUSEUM.DE

ÖFFNUNGSZEITEN:
MONTAG – FREITAG
10:00 – 17:00 H
SAMS. GESCHLOSSEN
SONNTAG
11:00 – 17:00 H

MUSEUM FÜR DRUCKKUNST
NONNENSTR. 38
04229 LEIPZIG

EIN MUSEUM ZUM ANFASSEN UND MITMACHEN. 500 JAHRE
DRUCKGESCHICHTE AUF VIER ETAGEN IN WERKSTATT-
ATMOSPHÄRE ERLEBEN.
FACHLEUTE FÜHREN DIE HISTORISCHEN MASCHINEN
JEDERZEIT VOR

MUSEUM FÜR DRUCKKUNST
NONNENSTR. 38
04229 LEIPZIG

MARTIN 07
MAJOOR: 11
HELVETICA 06
WAS 2–
A MISTAKE 6

MARTIN MAJOOR : HELVETICA WAS A MISTAKE
WERKPLAATS TYPOGRAFIE — 07/11/06 FROM 2 TO 6 PM
POSTER: GUILLAUME MOJON

The Corridor
28.02 —
09.04.2009

Forms of Inquiry:
The Architecture of
Critical Graphic Design

curated by Zak Kyes

The Corridor
The Corridor is BolteLang's
project space for new commissions, site specific installations
and exhibitions. It is a space with
restricted dimensions, raised to
the main gallery only geographically and therefore completely
open to experimentation. The
inherent conflict between the
promise of infinite possibilities
and spatial limitation is at the core
of The Corridor.

Forms of Inquiry
at The Corridor
Forms of Inquiry: The Architecture
of Critical Graphic Design curated
by Zak Kyes

Forms of Inquiry presents a group
of contemporary, international
graphic designers who base their
work in critical investigation.
The exhibition features works that
have originated as self-propelled
inquiry, either professional or personal, and have been developed
into a myriad of media and forms.
The exhibition expands as its travels, continually emphasising local
research and sites for exchange.

The fifth constellation of Forms
of Inquiry includes several new
commissions and a four-week
public programme, opening
simultaneously at Archizoom,
Lausanne on 89 February at 07???
and at The Corridor at BolteLang,
Zurich on 27 February 2009 where
a selection of Forms of Inquiry
prints will be on view.

Forms of Inquiry
contributors
Åbäke, Julia Born & Alexandra
Bachzetsis, Laurenz Brunner,
Sara De Bondt, deValence,
Dexter Sinister, Paul Elliman,
Experimental Jetset, Martin
Frostner & Jonas Williamsson,
Ryan Gander, Liam Gillick,
James Goggin, Francesca Grassi,
Jonathan Hares, Will Holder,
Hudson-Powell, David Keshavjee
& Julien Tavelli, Hoon Kim,
Kasia Korczak, Kueng Caputo,
Jürg Lehni, Urs Lehni & Lex Trüb,
Xiao Mage & Cheng Zi, Karel
Martens & David Bennewith,
Metahaven, Mevis en Van
Deursen, John Morgan, NORM,
Radim Peško, Project Projects,
Manuel Raeder, TASK, Emmet
Byrne, Alex DeArmond & Jon
Sueda, Cornel Windlin, Michael
Worthington

Public Program
FOUR DAYS IN THE FORM OF
AN INQUIRY, a four-week public
program curated by Nicole Udry
will take place at Archizoom in
Lausanne. See archizoom.epfl.ch
for more information.

Opening
Friday 27 February, 5-7 pm
The exhibition runs from
28 February – 9 April 2009

Open during gallery opening
hours and by appointment.

For further information
please contact:

BolteLang: info@boltelang.com
+41 44 273 00 10

www.boltelang.com
www.formsofinquiry.com
archizoom.epfl.ch

[01|02]

Zensur in der Kunst?
Neue Mechanismen und Strategien
5. und 6. Dezember 2008

Eine Tagung der Akademie Schloss Solitude,
des Hospitalhofs Stuttgart und des
Württembergischen Kunstvereins Stuttgart

EINFÜHRUNG
Nicht erst der Karikaturenstreit und der Streit
um die Berliner Inszenierung von Mozarts
„Idomeneo" machen darauf aufmerksam, dass
Zensur in allen Bereichen künstlerischer
Produktion, Vermittlung und Rezeption statt-
findet. So vielfältig die Formen der künstleri-
schen Betätigung heute sind, so vielfältig
sind auch die Formen ihrer Beschränkung und
Selbstbeschränkung. Die Tagung lädt zu
einer neuen Verständigung über den Wert der
Kunstfreiheit ein.

gefördert durch: KARIN ABT-STRAUBINGER **Stiftung** Baden-Württemberg STUTTGART

Zensur in der Kunst?
Neue Mechanismen und Strategien
5. und 6. Dezember 2008

Eine Tagung der Akademie Schloss Solitude,
des Hospitalhofs Stuttgart und des
Württembergischen Kunstvereins Stuttgart

—
L2M3
Sascha Lobe, Itxaso Mezzacasa

[01] Zensur in der Kunst

Poster for a congress at the Württemberg
Art Association.

Client / Publisher Württembergischer
Kunstverein Stuttgart

—
L2M3
Ina Bauer, Sascha Lobe

[02] Weder Entweder Noch Oder

Poster for a group exhibition at the Württemberg Art Association.

Client / Publisher Württembergischer
Kunstverein Stuttgart

[02]

HEY HO

[01] Press release Salon du livre 2009

Client / Publisher Galaade Éditions

[02] XVIII POSTER

Client XVIII BORDEAUX

[03] L'intraitable Beauté du Monde adresse à
     Barack Obama

Book from Edouard Glissant and Patrick
Chamoiseau addressed to Barack Obama.

Client Éditions Galaade Institut du Tout-Monde
Publisher Éditions Galaade

[01]

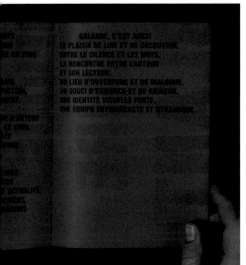

[03]

WHITENESSES

EINE AUSSTELLUNG VON
ARI KAKKINEN

MB FOTOGRAFIE

MARC BERVILLE
PROSPECTS

BRUNNENSTRASSE 7D (HINTERHAUS)
D-10119 BERLIN, DEUTSCHLAND
+49 30 54 78 58 61
WWW.MBPROSPECTS.COM
WWW.MBFOTOGRAFIE.COM
HELLO@MBPROSPECTS.COM

6. SEPTEMBER - 18. OKTOBER 2008
ERÖFFNUNG:
SAMSTAG, 6. SEPTEMBER, 19 UHR

design : Côme de Bouchony

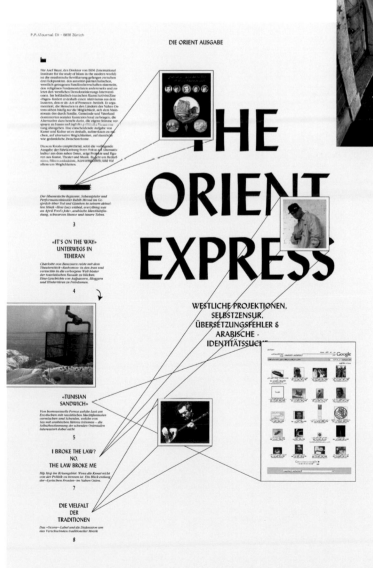

REMCO VAN BLADEL

[01] Shotgun Architecture by Justin Bennett

Poster for an album cover.

Publisher Onomatopee
Credits Photography and sonar images
by Justin Bennett

GLASHAUS
Gregor Huber & Ivan Sterzinger

[02] The Orient Express – Issue

Monthly newspaper for the culture centre
Rote Fabrik in Zürich.

Client / Publisher Rote Fabrik Zürich
Editors Gregor Huber, Ivan Sterzinger

[left page]

CÔME DE BOUCHONY

Ari Kakkinen – Whitenesses Poster

Folder poster sent as an invatation for Ari
Kakkinen's solo show at MB Prospects Gallery
in Berlin.

Client MB Prospects

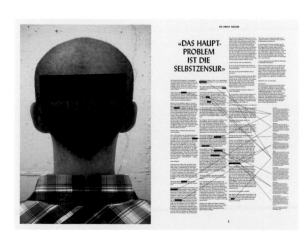

RAFFINERIE AG FÜR GESTALTUNG

[01]

[04]

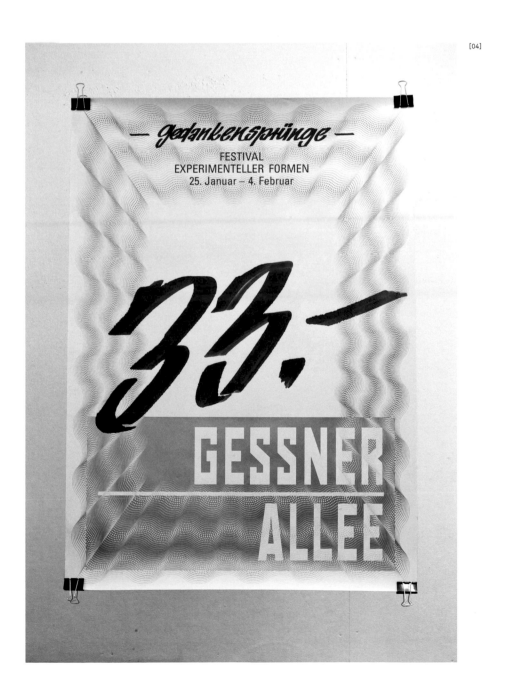

[left page]

SUPERBÜRO

Swiss Poster – Jungfrau Region (Front)

Poster about the Jungfrau region
published in *Wallpaper**.

Client / Editor / Publisher Wallpaper* Magazine on behalf
of Switzerland Tourism
Credits Photography by Stefan Hofmann, ph7

ANDREW WREN &
PHILIPPE EGGER / FAGETA

[01] **Swiss Poster – Jungfrau Region (Back)**

Poster about the Jungfrau region
published in *Wallpaper**.

Client / Editor / Publisher Wallpaper* Magazine on behalf
of Switzerland Tourism
Credits Art direction by Andrew Wren / Design by
Philippe Egger / Project managment by Mark
Stobbs / Project coordination by Carly Gray

KATJA GRETZINGER

[02–03] **European Kunsthalle Nov 2009**

Client European Kunsthalle
Credits Images copyrights: European Kunsthalle /
The Artists

[01]

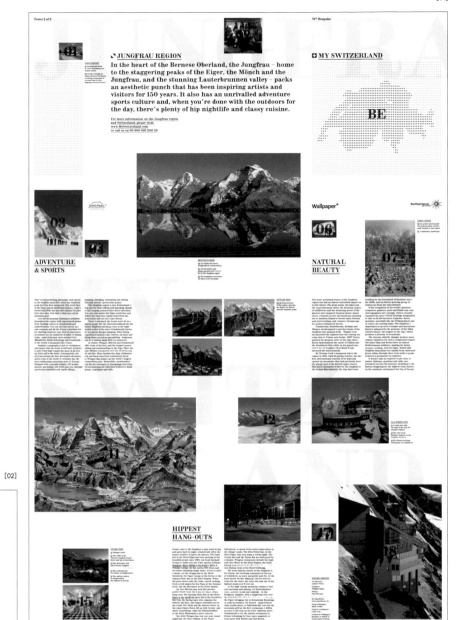

[02]

EUROPEAN
KUNSTHALLE
c/o Ebertplatz
#3
23. 10. – 18. 12. 2008

[03]

GEOMETRY

The use of basic geometric shapes, such as triangles and circles, and of primary colours in graphic design always represents a reaction against romanticism and naturalism. The geometry of the 1960s (Op art) favoured well-defined shapes over ornamental design, cold colours over earthy colours, and abstract forms over organic ones. Today, graphic designers still use a serial approach. They employ redundant forms and patterns – and this not just in the design of logos. Graphic designers experiment with perspectives, lines and transparency in a formal manner, and quote the halftone images used in Op art works. Works which remind us of Paco Rabanne coexist alongside mirror-image diamonds, optical illusions, solarisation effects, stroboscope logos, metal patterns, sequencers and moiré patterns such as those by Victor Vasarely. Basic geometric forms and crystalline structures are often mixed with structures from photography that are clearly influenced by the fantastic realism of the 1960s and 1970s.

TOAN VU-HUU

[01]   A CHACUN SES ETRANGERS ?

Poster for an exhibition tracing images of immigrants from 1871 to 2008 in Germany and France.

Client Cité nationale de l'histoire de l'immigration

L2M3
Sascha Lobe, Dirk Wachowiak

[02]   Wild Siganals

Poster for a group exhibition at the Württemberg Art Association.

Client / Publisher Württembergischer Kunstverein Stuttgart

[02]

[01]

Zbyněk Baladrán
Michael Beutler
Luca Buvoli
Simon Dybbroe Møller
Cyprien Gaillard
Dionisio González
Konsortium
Ciprian Mureșan
Deimantas Narkevicius
Veit Stratmann

FUSION//CONFUSION
12.01. – 30.03.2008

Di bis So 10 bis 18 Uhr, Fr bis 21 Uhr

Museum Folkwang

Kahrstraße 16
45128 Essen

www.museum-folkwang.de

Die Ausstellung wurde ermöglicht durch den Folkwang-Museumsverein e.V.
Mit freundlicher Unterstützung der Wall AG

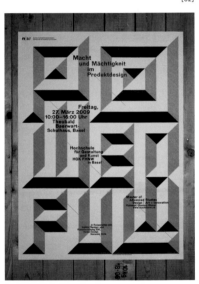

JUNG UND WENIG
Christopher Jung, Tobias Wenig &
Pascal Storz

[01]   FUSION // CONFUSION

Poster for the *Fusion // Confusion* exhibition
at the Folkwang Museum in Essen.

Client Folkwang Museum, Essen, Germany

STUDIO SPORT
Ronnie Fueglister & Martin Stoecklin

[02]   Powerful

Silkscreen poster and flyer for the design conference *Powerful* at the University of Art and
Design Basel, Switzerland.

Client / Publisher / Editor Dominic Sturm, HGK Basel

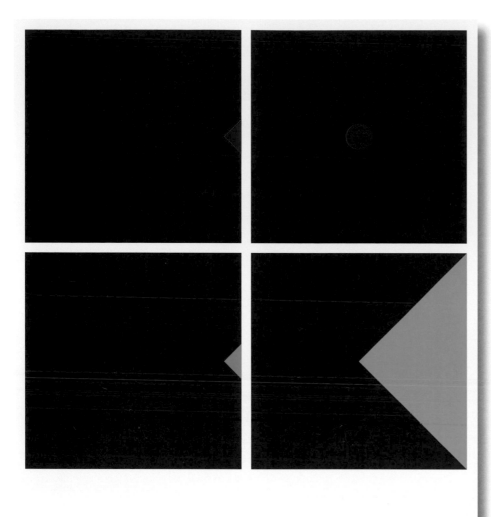

- G A L L E R Y -

Ontwerper Henk Cornelissen / **Lokatie** Stadsgalerij Breda
Datum 24 mei t/m 29 juni 2008 / **Open** vr/za/zo 13-17 uur

TOKO DESIGN

Young Guns Awards 2008

Poster invitations for the Young Guns Awards
2008. The topic *Quit in Style* is expressed in
5 confronting poster concepts, rude, funny and
in your face.

Client Droga5

Graphic Design Festival Breda

Two posters for the Graphic Design Festival
in Breda. The first poster is a play on one
of the techniques graphic designer Henk
Cornelissen uses to create coincidences,
using dice. The second poster is research into
all the key dates in Henk's professional life
in search of a relationship between events
and their duration.

Client Graphic Design Festival Breda

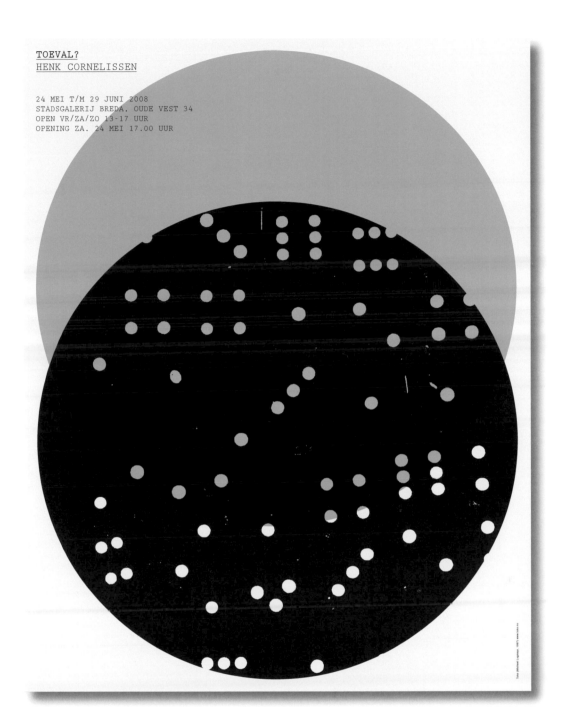

TOEVAL?
HENK CORNELISSEN

24 MEI T/M 29 JUNI 2008
STADSGALERIJ BREDA. OUDE VEST 34
OPEN VR/ZA/ZO 13-17 UUR
OPENING ZA. 24 MEI 17.00 UUR

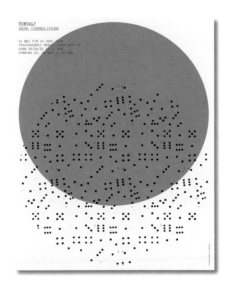

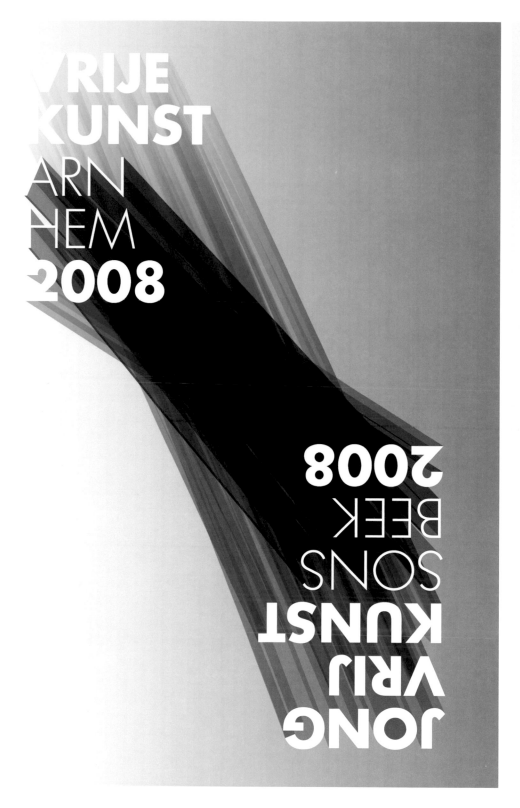

STUDIOSPASS
Jaron Korvinus & Daan Mens

[01] ArtEZ: Fine Arts graduation Identity

Identity, print campaign and catalogue
for the graduation show of the ArtEZ fine
art department and the follow-up show at
Sonsbeek 2008 Arts festival.

Client ArtEZ Hogeschool Voor de Kunsten

TOBIAS ROETTGER

[02] NOW Poster

Client ACMI

ZIGMUNDS LAPSA

[03] Dan Flavin poster

Poster for artist Dan Flavin's exhibition at
Tate Modern.

ZAK KLAUCK

[04] Future of Graphic Design

Poster based on a study from M.I.T. on how
knowledge is communicated between hu-
mans in graphic design.

IMJ
Jae-Hyouk Sung

[05] Yokoo Tadanori Poster Exhibition

Poster for Yokoo Tadanori Poster Exhibition.

Client Zero-One Design Center
and Japan Foundation Seoul

[01|02]

[03]

Level 5: Idea and object
Room 6

TATE

[04]

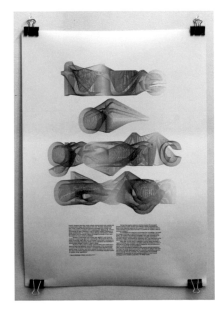

[05]

STANDPUNTEN.

ANDERS
KIJKEN NAAR
DE COLLECTIE
MODERNE
KUNST.

centraal
museum

UITNODIGING.

VRIJDAG
15 FEB 2008
1600 UUR.

centraal
museum

De directeur van het Centraal Museum Utrecht
nodigt u van harte uit voor de opening van de
tentoonstelling

STANDPUNTEN.
ANDERS KIJKEN NAAR
DE COLLECTIE MODERNE KUNST.
op 15 februari 2007 om 16.00 uur
in het Centraal Museum.

De opening wordt verricht door Hans Goedkoop,
historicus en criticus, bij het grote publiek bekend als
presentator van de televisieprogramma's De Kunst en
Andere Tijden.

Het Centraal Museum toont met Standpunten
de collectie moderne kunst in een nieuwe, verfrissende
context. Thema's als massacultuur, politiek, vrijheid
en elite vormen het vertrekpunt voor een
experimentele kijk op de collectie, waarbij de
traditionele kunsthistorische kaders worden losgelaten.
Zeven hedendaagse kunstenaars voegen er actuele en
persoonlijke standpunten aan toe, door muurtekeningen
te maken die een relatie aan gaan met de getoonde
kunstwerken.
De tentoonstelling is te zien tot medio 2009.

CENTRAAL MUSEUM.
Nicolaaskerkhof 10, Utrecht, tel: 030 2362362
www.centraalmuseum.nl
open: dinsdag t/m zondag 11.00-17.00 uur
gesloten: maandag, 25 december, 1 januari en 30 april

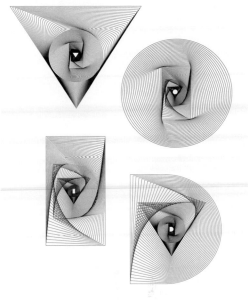

LESLEY MOORE

[01]   Standpoints

The aim of the exhibition was to give an alternative way of viewing the modern art collection, seen from seven different standpoints. The poster visualises quite literally the title. A 3-dimensional typographic composition was designed to show different and impossible perspectives in one image. The image has a subtle reference to the Dutch master of graphic illusion M.C. Escher.

Client Centraal Museum Utrecht

[02]   Rietvelds' Slender Space Sculptures and other creations of the avant-garde

Poster for an art exhibition inspired by the *De Stijl* movement.

Client Centraal Museum Utrecht

[03]   VOID

Poster inspired by *Droste-effect* images. *Droste-effect* is the term used to describe images that repeat themselves ad infinitum within the picture plan.

[05]

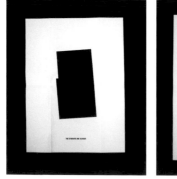

**ALINA GÜNTER &
COBOI / Katharina Reidy**

[01, 05]   The Students are alright /
            Kunstdiplom 07 HKB

Flyers and Posters as invitations for
the diploma exhibition of the Bern
University of Arts.

Client Bern University of Arts

**COBOI / Katharina Reidy &
FAGETA / Philippe Egger &
Adeline Mollard**

[02]   Bad Bonn Kilbi 2009 Poster

Identity for the Bad Bonn Kilbi Festival in
Düdingen, Switzerland.

—
MIND DESIGN

[03] Belmacz Poster 2

Poster for a London-based avantgarde
jewellery company.

Client Belmacz
Credits Photographer: Ram Shergill

—
SERIAL CUT™
Sergio Del Puerto

[04] GEOMETRICAL MESS

Tee-shirt design.

Client Vicelona
Credits Illustration by Miss Minou / Model: Bachicho

KAZUNARI HATTORI

[01|02|03]

[04|05|06]

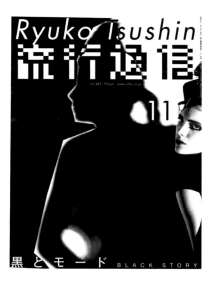

[07|08|09]

開館15周年記念

ハンス・アルプ展

"われわれは
香りよき人間粒では
なかったか？"
Hans Arp

Hans Arp:
Works from the Collections of the
ARP MUSEUM, Bahnhof Rolandseck

2005年4月5日（火）〜6月26日（日）

川村記念美術館

Kawamura Memorial Museum of Art
千葉県佐倉市坂戸631　0120-498-130
http://www.dic.co.jp/museum/

開館時間：午前9時30分→午後5時　＊入館は午後4時30分まで
休館日：月曜日　＊ただし、5/2（月）は開館
入館料：一般1200円（1000円）
　　　　大高生・70歳以上1000円（800円）
　　　　中小生400円（300円）
　　　　＊常設展もご覧いただけます。＊（　）内は団体［20名以上］料金
主催：川村記念美術館（大日本インキ化学工業株式会社）／東京新聞
共催：アルプ美術館バーンホフ・ローランズエック
後援：ドイツ連邦共和国大使館／千葉県／千葉県教育委員会／
　　　佐倉市／佐倉市教育委員会
協力：全日本空輸株式会社／日本貨物航空株式会社

2005
2006
Deutschland
in Japan
日本におけるドイツ
ドイツ

[01]

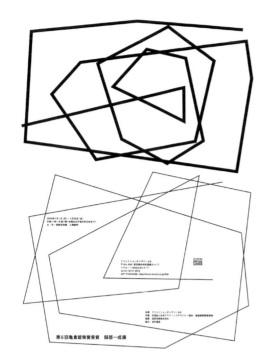

第6回亀倉雄策賞受賞 服部一成展

[03]

—

KAZUNARI HATTORI

[01]   Hattori Exhibition Poster

[02]   ADC Exhibition Poster

[04]   7seven Poster

—

KATJA GRETZINGER

[03]   Zurich Jazz Orchestra – New Plans

Album cover for the Zürich
Jazz Orchestra playing the music of
Rainer Tempel.

Client Zürich Jazz Orchestra

SEVEN

K.HATTORI

[01]

 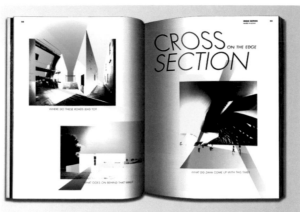 

LESLEY MOORE

[01]   Mark – Another Architecture

Design for bimonthly magazine, focusing
on architecture and exploring its boundaries.

Client / Publisher Mark Publishers
Editor Robert Thiemann, Arthur Wortmann, David
Keuning

MADS FREUND BRUNSE / ECAL

[02]   From Diseases to Side Effects

Installation and poster series analysing
medicine's side effects and their antidotes
using graphic links.

ESAM LEE

[03]   Flyer poster

Sampling and reinterpretation of several
Korean restaurant advertising flyers.

[02]

[03]

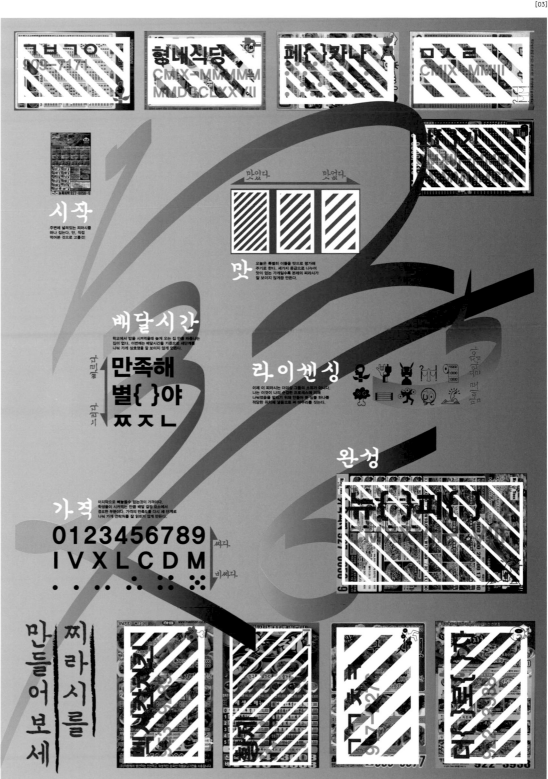

NIESSEN &
DE VRIES

Richard Niessen and Esther de Vries are partners in life and work. While they both studied at the Gerrit Rietveld Academy in Amsterdam, Niessen graduating in 1996, de Vries two years later in 1998, it was not until a few years later that they met for the first time. With friends in common, de Vries took over Niessen's workspace and so began their relationship.

Married in 2005, the couple decided to work together when they realised they were always discussing their work when they got home, and in 2008 they set up their studio, *Niessen & de Vries*, in Amsterdam.

The design duo tends to work with cultural clients. They create books in collaboration with artists, such as Jennifer Tee and Gabriel Lester, and publicity for galleries and museums. These include the Stedelijk and the Van Gogh museums, both in Amsterdam, as well as the Gemeentemuseum in The Hague.

Self-initiated projects are, however, also a very important part of their work and Niessen & de Vries cite their exhibition, *TM-City*, as their favourite project to date. The 2007 exhibition, held in Chaumont, France at the time of the International Poster and Design Festival, saw the team create a city out of 150 existing pieces of Niessen's work: flyers were stacked to form skyscrapers, posters laid out to become parks. Fully traversable, people could walk down the streets, which are named after people who inspire them, from Richard Rogers to Eduardo Paolozzi. TM stands for Typographic Masonry, the term that Niessen uses to describe his work.

In 1998, while still at the Rietveld Academy, de Vries started a small publishing house, when she made the book *Photos*, with a selection of black-and-white photographs taken by Auke de Vries. The award-winning book sold out. Little by little, new titles are added to the publisher's list.

Both Dutch, Niessen was born in Edam-Volendam in 1972, De Vries in The Hague in 1974.

NIESSEN & DE VRIES

[01]   Stedelijk Museum New Year's Card

New Year card using patterns based on the previous year's annual report from the museum.

Client Stedelijk Museum
Credits Print by Rob Stolk

[02]   Res Artis 11th General Meeting

Identity including posters, booklet, buttons and stickers for an art event.

Client Res Artis

[03]   SNCF

Poster visualising the slogan of the French railway company SNCF, celebrating its 70th anniversary.

Client SNCF

KAZUNARI HATTORI

Flag Posters
Cake Posters

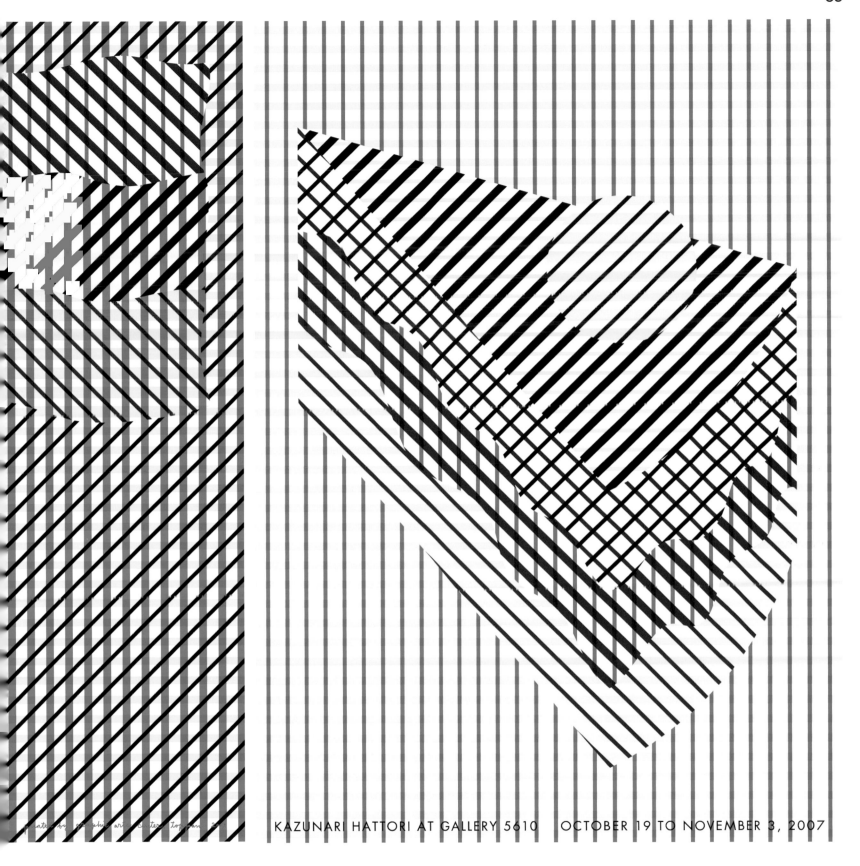

KAZUNARI HATTORI AT GALLERY 5610   OCTOBER 19 TO NOVEMBER 3, 2007

[01]

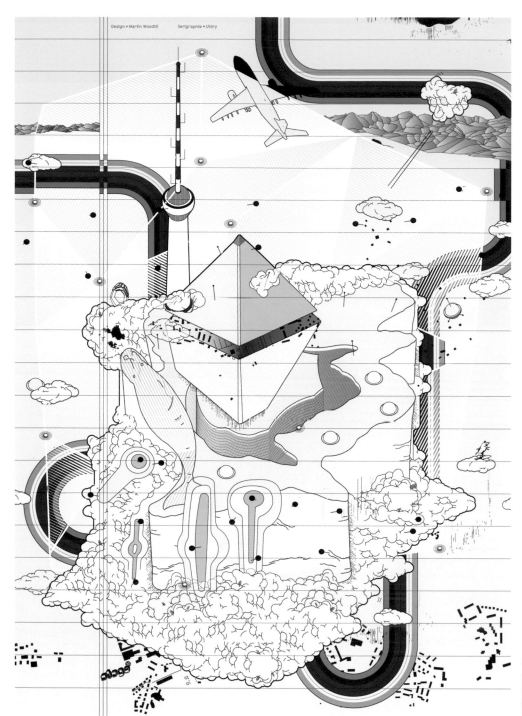

[02]

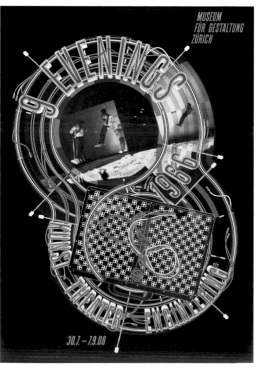

—
MARTIN WOODTLI

[01] <u>Kunst vor Ort Die Stadtgalerie
Bern 1999–2006</u>

Martin Woodtli was invited by Stadtgalerie
Bern to design a bill/poster for the publication *Kunst vor Ort*, which can be folded and
then used as a book jacket/cover.

Client Stadtgalerie Bern
Publisher Editionfink / Beate Engel, Stadtgalerie Bern

[02] <u>9 Evenings 1966: Kunst, Theater und Engineering</u>

Poster for an art exhibition addressing the
interaction of creative performance and
technical progress.

Client Museum für Gestaltung Zürich

[03] <u>VideoEx 2008</u>

Poster for Videoex , international experimental film and video festival.

Client Kunstraum Walcheturm

23. MAI – 01. JUNI 2008

VIDEOEX ▶ INTERNATIONALES
EXPERIMENTAL FILM & VIDEO FESTIVAL

KANONENGASSE 20 ZURICH
WWW.VIDEOEX.CH

17-27
MAI
2007

INTERNATIONALES
EXPERIMENTALFILM
UND
VIDEO FESTIVAL
ZÜRICH
KUNSTRAUM
WALCHETURM
KANONENGASSE 20
8004
ZÜRICH

SPECIAL I:

SPECIAL II:

SPECIAL III:
SOUND, PIXEL AND N

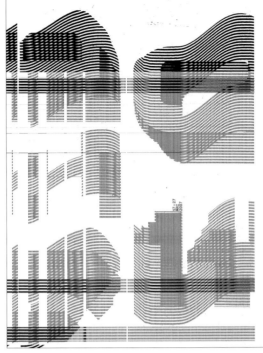

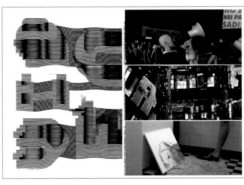

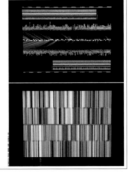

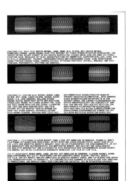

—
MARTIN WOODTLI

VideoEx

Newspaper for the international experimental film and video festival Videoex.

Client Kunstraum Walcheturm

BURRI – PREIS
Susanne Burri

HGKL DIPL.07

Orientation plan for a diploma exhibition of the Academy for Design and Art Luzern.

Client Hochschule Luzern – Design&Kunst

SANDRA KASSENAAR

[02] Here I am, keep me in mind

Self-initiated publication addressing the application of colour in the context of political content, self-concept and identification.

VON B UND C
Barbara Hahn & Christine Zimmermann

[03] Women's Phone – Adjektivische Skalen

[04, 05] Women's Phone – Formalästhetische Analyse

Series of posters for the scientific study *Women's Phone*.

Client Deutsche Telekom Laboratories
Credits Developed for Women's Phone, Deutsche Telekom Laboratories, Direction by Prof. Dr. Gesche Joost

WHY NOT SMILE
Hoon Kim

[06] Audio Signals

Publication showing how sound visualization can be applied to the structure of a book. The information on the cover contains different pitches generating different line quantities with different thicknesses.

[01]
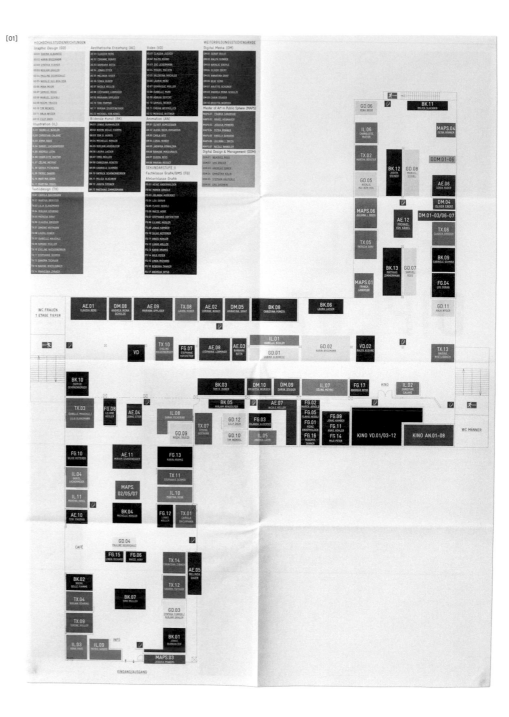

[02]

[03|04]

Women's Phone: **Adjektivische Skalen II**

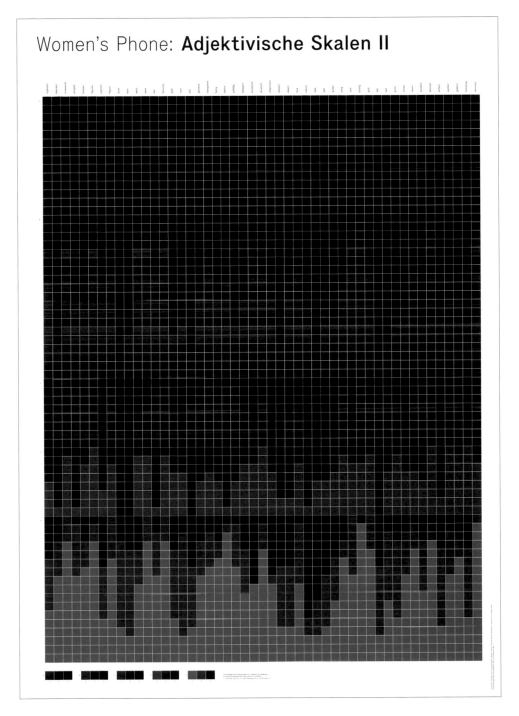

Women's Phone: **Analyse Farbe**

[05]

Women's Phone: **Analyse Struktur**

[06]

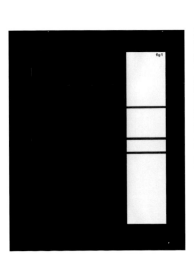

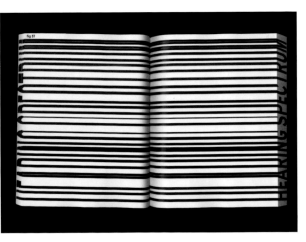

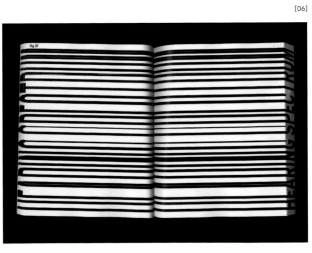

http://www.aec.at
http://www.convivionetwork.net
http://www.densitydesign.org
http://www.desphilosophy.com
http://www.designresearchsociety.org
http://www.digicult.it
http://www.doorsofperception.com
http://www.experimenta.org
http://www.forumforthefuture.org.uk
http://www.hexagram.ca
http://www.idonline.com
http://www.ijdesign.org
http://www.informationdesign.org
http://www.interaction-design.org
http://www.mediamatic.net
http://www.neural.it
http://nextd.org
http://www.noemalab.org
http://nova.ilsole24ore.com
http://rhizome.org
http://www.sciam.com
http://sigchi.org
http://siggraph.org
http://www.stockexchangeofvisions.org
http://www.ted.com
http://www.viridiandesign.org
http://www.wired.com
http://www.xcult.ch

http://www.apple.com/iphone
http://www.frogdesign.com
http://www.design.philips.com
http://www.global.yamaha.com/design/index.html
http://www.ideo.com
http://www.interactiondesign-lab.com
http://www.laptop.org
http://lawsofsimplicity.com
http://www.loewe.de

OGGETTI COLLOQUIALI
COLLOQUIAL OBJECTS

http://www.maedastudio.com
http://www.media.mit.edu
http://safe.mercedes-benz.co.uk
http://www.nintendo.com/ds
http://www.nose.ch
http://www.soundbug.biz
http://www.alistapart.com
http://www.bfgf.de
http://hello.eboy.com
http://www.ertdfgcvb.ch
http://infosthetics.com
http://wwww.oneone-studio.com
http://sodaplay.com
http://www.visualcomplexity.com
http://www.yugop.com
http://www.mutado.com
http://www.warprecords.com

AMBIE
IMME

MASTER OF ARTS SUPSI IN
—INTERACTION DESIGN

Esplora il mondo dell'interaction design visitando la collezione di alcuni dei riferimenti più significativi e attuali.

Explore the world of interaction design by visiting the collection of some of the most significative and updated references

http://www.colourlovers.com
http://www.designerblog.it
http://www.designtaxi.com
http://www.eff.org
http://www.idearium.org
http://www.dataisnature.com
http://www.generatorx.no
http://www.gizmodo.it
http://www.itsnicethat.com
http://www.kloonigames.com/blog
http://makezine.com
http://www.newitalianblood.com
http://www.pixelsumo.com
http://www.shapeshifters.net
http://spamnation.info
http://swissmiss.typepad.com
http://www.we-make-money-not-art.com

http://developer.apple.com
http://www.docomolabs-usa.com
http://www.research.ibm.com
http://www.merl.com
http://research.microsoft.com
http://www.incx.nec.co.jp/robot
http://research.nokia.com
http://www.parc.com
http://www.research.philips.com
http://techresearch.intel.com
http://www.telecomitalia.com
http://www.w3.org
http://www.artemide.com
http://www.bang-olufsen.com
http://www.bticino.com
http://www.lge.com
http://www.jamo.com
http://www.microvision.com
http://www.motorola.com
http://www.nintendo.it
http://www.nttdocomo.com
http://www.osram-os.com
http://www.samsung.com
http://www.sonyericsson.com

PROGETTARE IL FUTURO
DESIGNING THE FUTURE

http://www.arduino.cc
http://artsoftware.org
http://www.cycling74.com
http://www.dynamicdiagrams.com
http://www.makingthings.com
http://onecm.com/sketches
http://www.processing.org
http://www.tinker.it
http://www.troikatronix.com/isadora.html
http://vvvv.org

PROTESI COMUNICATIVE
COMMUNICATIONS PROTHESES

Metropolis 1927/Fritz Lang
Mon oncle 1958/Jacques Tati
Playtime 1967/Jacques Tati
2001: A Space Odyssey 1968/Stanley
Star Wars 1977 '80 '83/George Lucas
Tron 1982/Steven M. Lisberger
Blade Runner 1982/Ridley Scott
Brazil 1985/Terry Gilliam
Luxo Jr. 1986/John Lasseter
Until the End of the World 1991/Wim
Strange Days 1995/Kathryn Bigelow
Johnny Mnemonic 1995/Robert Long
Toy Story 1995/John Lasseter
Nirvana 1997/Gabriele Salvatores
Gattaca 1997/Andrew Niccol
The Matrix 1999/Andy and Larry Wa
AI: Artificial Intelligence 2001/Steve
Minority Report 2002/Steven Spielbe

RI
FU

—
C2F
Cybu Richli & Fabienne Burri

Master of Arts in Interaction Design

Folded poster for the Interaction Design
program of the University of Lugano.

Client SUPSI University of Applied Sciences and Arts
of Southern Switzerland

//www.bashiba.com
//www.cliostraat.com
//www.gysin-vanetti.com
//www.hager.it
//www.iguzzini.com
//www.interactivearchitecture.org
//ioagency.com
//www.jung.de
//www.limiteazero.net

RSIVI
IRONMENTS

//naturalinteraction.org
//www.philipperahm.com
//senseable.mit.edu
//www.sensitivespacesystem.com
//www.somfy.it
//www.distantair.com
//www.learnlakenona.com
//www.spent2000.com
//www.tonicgroup.com/versioncity/home.htm
//universe.daylife.com
//secondlife.com
//www.virtualenvironments.info

http://www.cfsd.org.uk
http://www.designcouncil.org.uk/en/About-Design/
        Design-Disciplines/Service-design-by-Bill-Hollins
http://www.dba.org.uk
http://www.technologyandsocialaction.org
http://www.theoscarproject.org
http://www.enginegroup.co.uk
http://www.experientia.com
http://www.icscarsharing.it
http://future.iftf.org
http://www.ideaplay.org.uk
http://www.treehugger.com
http://www.unep.fr/en
http://worldcarshare.com
http://www.worldchanging.com
http://www.2c.nl
http://www.blinkx.com
http://del.icio.us
http://flffound.com
http://210.212.236.212/akshaya
http://www.google.com
http://www.kazaa.com
http://www.linkedin.com
http://www.myspace.com
http://www.skype.com
http://www.tveyes.com
http://www.youtube.com
http://www.wikipedia.org

SERVIZI INNOVATIVI
INNOVATIVE SERVICES

INTERAGIRE SOSTENIBILE
SUSTAINABLE INTERACTION

BISOGNI
EEDS

BON BON BÜRO

[01] Bon Bon Büro für HATE.

Poster presenting a mathematical system
that is filled with different fragments of
fictional and non-fictonal statements/signs.

Client HATE. Magazin

[02] Kartografie der Königsrouten

Book and posters as a hommage to a canon
of forms of architecture using photography,
graphics and typography to create new
forms of space, and define a new understanding of design.

[01]

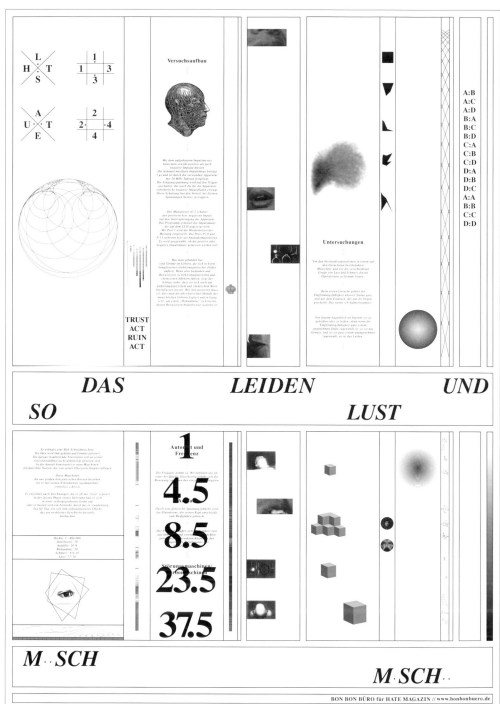

[02]

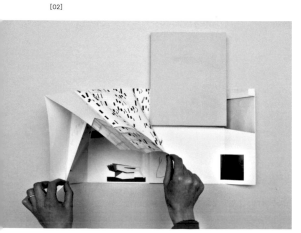
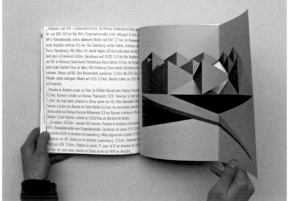
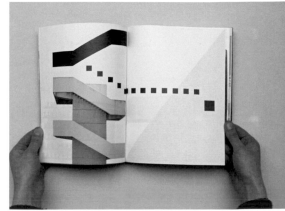

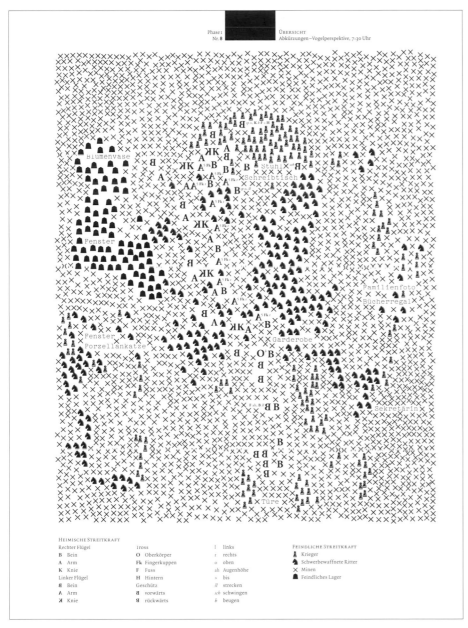

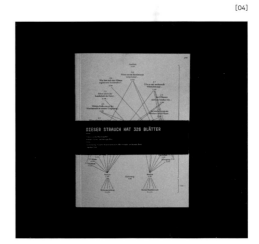

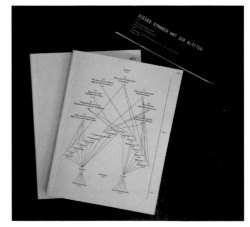

COBOI
Katharina Reidy

[03] Fürst Geherich fürchte dich nicht!

Part of the Diploma work Hochschule der
Künste Bern HKB.

PIROL
Simone Farner
in collaboration with Krispin Heé

[04] Dieser Strauch hat 326 Blaetter

Book in two volumes as experimental scientific Diploma work about the hazelnut tree.

Client Diplomarbeit HKB

[01]

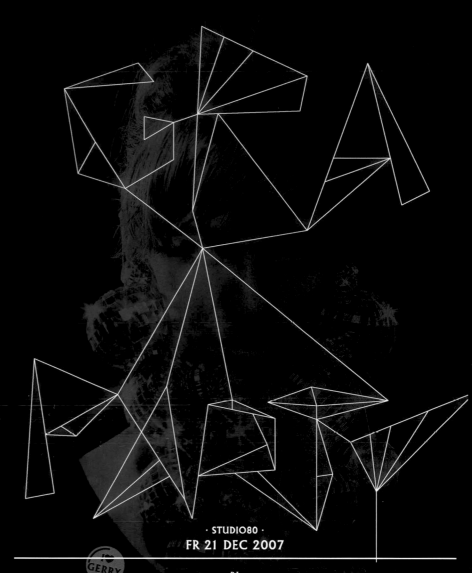

· STUDIO80 ·
FR 21 DEC 2007

GERRY

GRA THE LAST NIGHT
PARTY OPEN 23.00–05.00
ENTRY €7 · NO BEARD €10
REMBRANDTPLEIN 17
PRESALE WWW.GRAPARTY.COM

DJ
**OSLO HILTON
VITAMIN K
RIK**

VJ LIVE
GINTA TINTA PERFORMANCES
SJOCOSJON WALLPAINTING
JAKOP BY GRA STUDENTS

· BRING YOUR BEARD ·

[02]

FRI-
SON

SINCE 1983
ROUTE DE LA FONDERIE, FRIBOURG
NEW! WWW.FRI-SON.CH

fríson

LU
DÈ
L'U
WV
WV

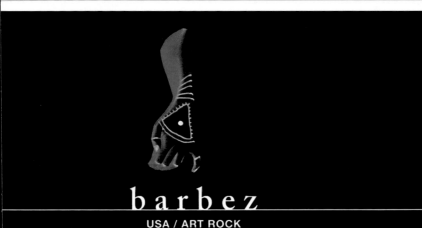

b a r b e z
USA / ART ROCK

+

sir richard bishop
USA / SOLO ACOUSTIC GUITAR

+

j victoria favorites
USA / ROB MILLS (FROM CLIMAX GOLDEN TWINS)

26	**JANVIER**	**2009**
10 CHF	CO-PROD KAB/CAVE 12	
4, PL. DES VOLONTAIRES	1204 GENÈVE	
LEKAB.	CH	
CAVE12.	ORG	

---

light   ning
b   o   l.   t
(USA)   DRUM/BASS   THUNDER

but   ter   cup
m   e   a   l
p   o   l   i   s   h
(CH)   IMPROV   DRUMS   DUO

MERCREDI   19   **NOVEMBRE**   2008
DÈS 21H   12CHF   **CONCERT AU ZOO!**
L'USINE (KAB)   4,   PLACE DES VOLONTAIRES   1204   GENÈVE
WWW   LEKAB   CH

DIEGO FELLAY / ECAL

[01] Le graphiste 2.0

Poster and book addressing the relation of
the graphic designer and the world wide web.

DENNY BACKHAUS & PER TÖRNBERG

[02] GRA Party – Disco Edition

Promotion poster for a party.

Client GRA Party
Credits Photography by Semuel Souhuwat

BILLY BEN & ANNA HAAS

[03] Fri-Son 25th Anniversary

Promotion poster and merchandising for the
25th anniversary of the Fri-Son Club.

Client Fri-Son

FLORENCE TÉTIER

[04] Barbez / Sir Richard Bishop Flyer

Client Usine / Genève

[05] Lightning Bolt Flyer

Client Usine / Genève

[01|02|03]

LT404

LT404

LT407

—n°1
"soundtrack" for Pierrot le Fou
from Jean Luc Godard featuring
Anna Karina & Jean Paul Belmondo
performed by:

Letraset

MULTIMEDI

KASSETTER, CDRER, ZINES, BÖCKER OCH ANDRA SAKER.

16.00

22.00

FÖRSÄLJNING AV SAKER FRÅN:

PUSH THE BUTTON
UTMARKEN
RELEASE THE BATS
KLOROFYLL KASSETTER
DOMINO

MUSIK AV:

PWR (GBG)
NIGHT PIANO

[04|05]

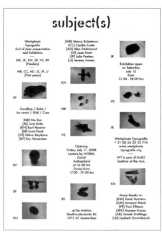

—
LETRA
Marco Balesteros

[01]   Pierrot le Fou Love Letter letra

Poster as a homage to Jean Luc Godard's
Pierrot le Fou.

[03]   Wonder Years WTX + EXD-A Party

Poster promoting the launch of the book
Wonder Years.

Client Werkplaats Typografie
Credits Typeface design by Radim Pesko White tape
WTX design by Na Kim

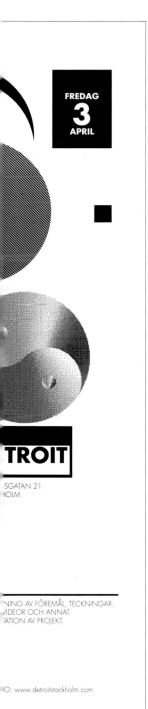

LETRA
Marco Balesteros

[04] Hong Kong Dong Poster

Poster designed to promote Hong Kong
Dong's live concert in the WT basement.

Client WT / S P E E L P L A A T S

[05] End of Year graduation WT 08 invitation

Invitation for graduation show and exhibition using objects found in the second year
students' desks.

Client Werkplaats Typografie

RASMUS EMANUEL SVENSSON

[02] Detroit poster

Poster advertising a night of music and visu-
als at the Detroit Gallery in Stockholm.

Client Detroit gallery

MUSEUM STUDIO

[01] Mask Print

Illustration collage and typeface for
clothing brand.

Client Sixpack France

MASH
James Brown & Ryan Psaila

[02] The Shiny Brights EP

CD packaging and poster for
The Shiny Brights.

Client The Shiny Brights
Credits Illustration by Peta Kruger

[01]

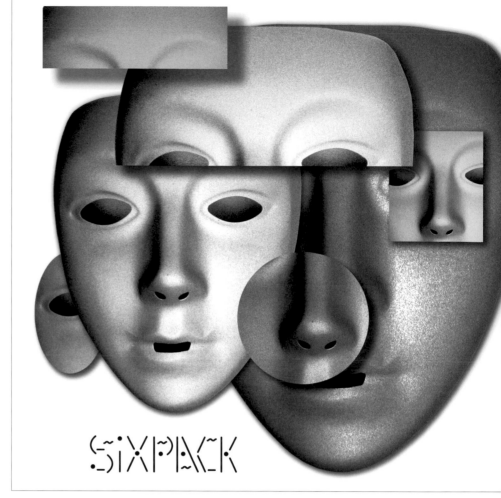

[02]

RASMUS EMANUEL SVENSSON

[03] Evergreen

Cover design for 12inch vinyl record.

Client The band pistol disco.
Publisher Celebrity lifestyle records

[04] Globe 13
[05] Globe 19
[06] Globe 27

Part of a series of digital collages
called *Globes.*

Client Futureclaw Magazine.

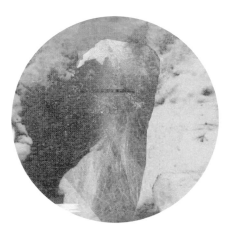
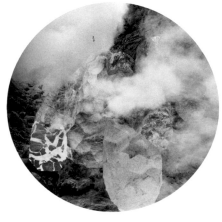

03

[04]

[05]

[06]

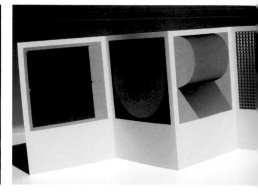

[01]

TOKO DESIGN

P. 102–103, 186—187

Partners in life and work, *Toko* are Eva Dijkstra and Michael Lugmayr.

Dijkstra was born in 1974 in Rotterdam, the Netherlands while Lugmayr was born in Krefeld, Germany in 1970, though he grew up in Venlo, the Netherlands. Today they are based in Sydney, Australia.

Dijkstra and Lugmayr met at the Academy of Fine Art and Design St. Joost, Breda in the Netherlands, where they graduated in 1999 and 1997, respectively. While Dijkstra tells us she chose graphic design over other art subjects for its diversity, Lugmayr explains: "Sometime during the early nineties I became fascinated by graffiti and the creative use of type. This fascination became serious when I realised you could actually make money by exploiting your hobby." "When I first got hold of some posters designed by *Studio Dumbar* for Zeebelt theatre and by *Opera* for Apollo Huis, I was sold," he adds.

Working at several agencies in the Netherlands and the United States, the studio eventually set up shop in 2001 under the name of 21" (21 inch), before changing the name to *Toko* in 2003.

Of their design process, *Toko* tell us: "We try to approach every project from a fresh perspective. In the process we try to forget all we have done before, to keep it exciting and surprising, and above all to create a space for a 'potential' experimental approach. We respect clients and their particular wishes but always try to challenge them to do something out of the ordinary."

Inspired by "more or less everything", from "art, architecture, a good book, music, travelling, visiting a gallery/museum to doing absolutely nothing," their clients to date include: The City of Sydney, Virgin Atlantic, UTS School of Architecture, the Architecture Institute Rotterdam, the Institute of Architecture Australia, the University of NSW, the cities of Rotterdam and The Hague, LAVA Architects, *MTV* and *The New York Times*.

[02]

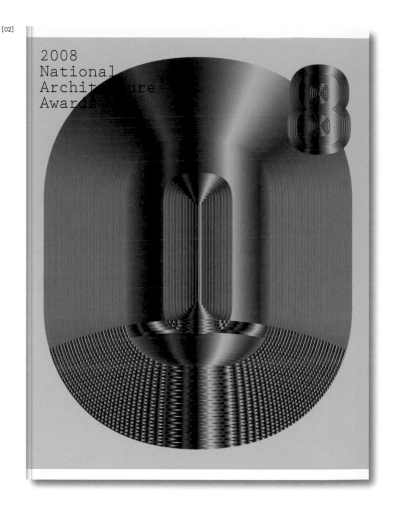

TOKO DESIGN

[01] Platform Exhibition

Exhibition and invitation design.
Client Faculty of Build Environment UNSW

[02] Identity 2008 National Architecture Awards, Australia

Book cover for the 2008 National Architecture Awards held in the City of Churches Adelaide.
Client Australian Institute of Architects

[03] 2008 Architecture Awards

Poster for the 2008 National Architecture Awards held in the City of Churches Adelaide.
Client Australian Institute of Architects

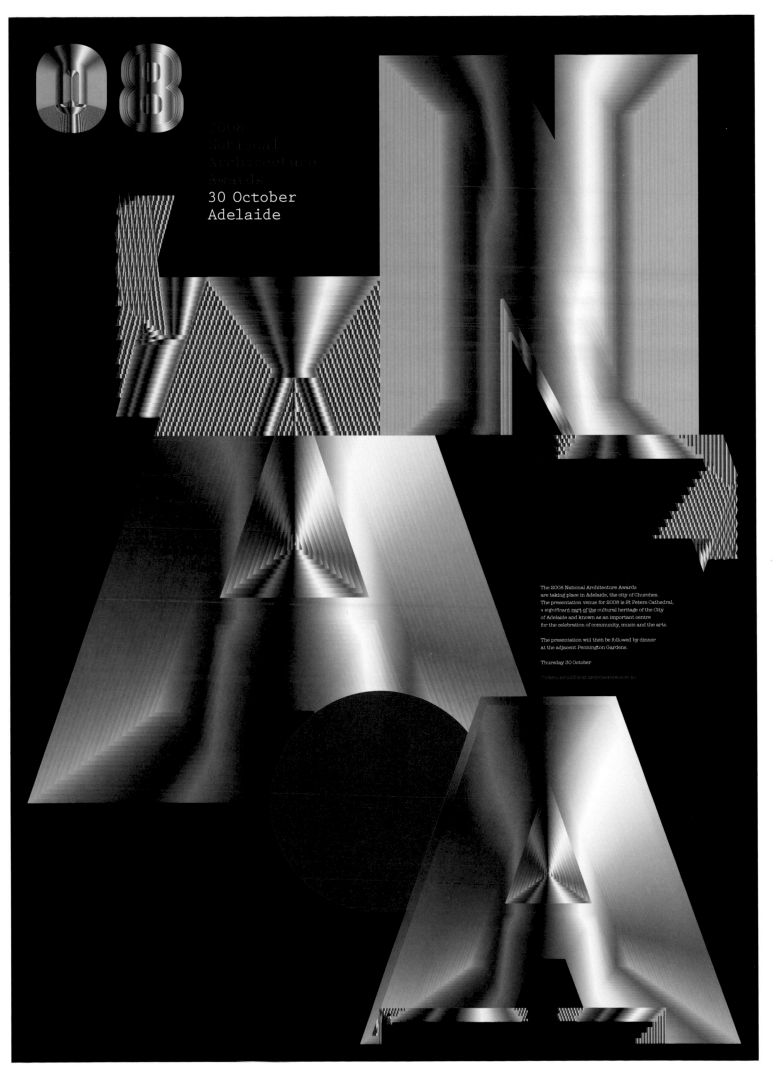

2008
National
Architecture
Awards
30 October
Adelaide

The 2008 National Architecture Awards
are taking place in Adelaide, the city of Churches.
The presentation venue for 2008 is St Peters Cathedral,
a significant part of the cultural heritage of the City
of Adelaide and known as an important centre
for the celebration of community, music and the arts.

The presentation will then be followed by dinner
at the adjacent Pennington Gardens.

Thursday 30 October

Tickets available at architecture.com.au

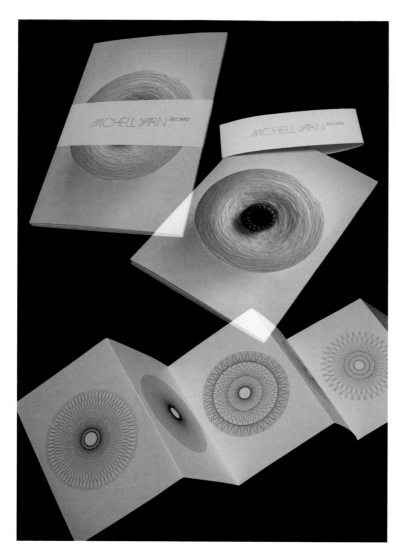

[03]

MASH
Darren Song

[01] Michell 1870 Yarn

Brochure promoting a brand.

Client Michell 1870
Credits Photography by Dom Roberts /
Art direction by Dom Roberts

MASH
James Brown & Dom Roberts
& Darren Song

[02] Clare Inc. Identity

Identity and stationery for a fashion
online retailer.

Client Claire Inc.

MARCUS KRAFT

[03] Musicology of Life

Vinyl single and CD design featuring a
booklet that shows a particular illustration
for each song – more or less abstract. The
outer format of the packaging is a memory
of my childhood: it has got the dimension of
a 7"-single-record.

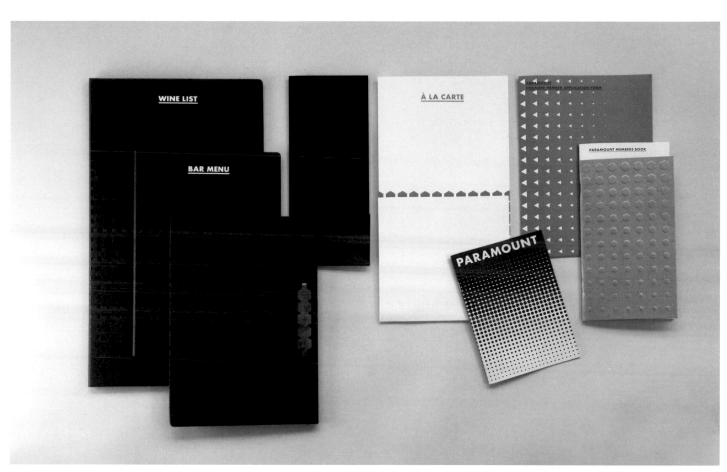

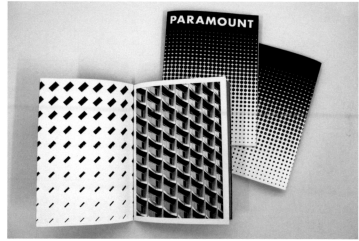

MIND DESIGN

Paramount Identity

Identity for a members club and events space located on one of London's first high rise buildings.

Client Paramount
Credits Interior Design by Tom Dixon /
Design Research Studio

[01]

[02]

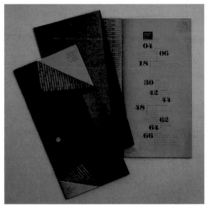  

JANINE REWELL

[01] Relative directions

Book addressing reading habits.

Client Personal / RISD

[02] Packaging music

Cover, packaging design and typeface for a CD album that contains funeral music from different cultures and tribes.

Client personal / RISD

JANINE REWELL & LOTTA NIEMINEN

[03] Tuli&Savu

Design and layout for the anniversary issue of a Finnish poetry magazine.

Client Nihil Interit & Univerity of Art and Design Helsinki
Publisher Nihil Interit

[01|04]

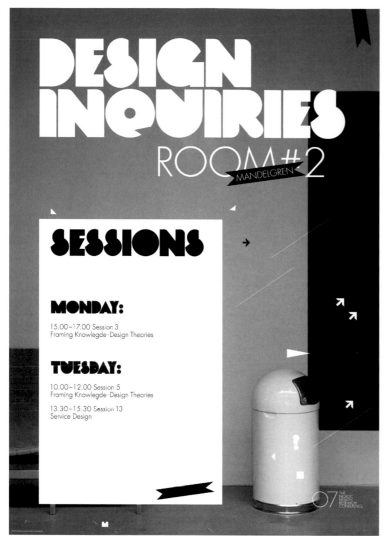

[02]

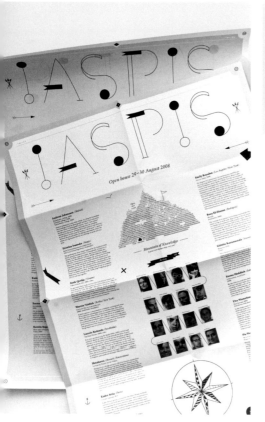

[03]

—
THEYGRAPHICS
Jiri Adamik-Novak & Fredrik Forsberg

[01]   Design Inquiries

Poster and illuminated sign for Nordic design research conference *Design Inquiries*.

[02]   The Iaspis Open House

Poster and program for The Iaspis Open House, 2008, combining self-made original typeface with simple navigation system inspired by old treasure maps.

^{Client} IASPIS, the International Artists' Studio Program, Sweden
^{Credits} Photography by Hana Roubickova

[03]   Anna-Maria Espinosa

CD packaging using collage, photography and illustration.

^{Client} Bonnier Music Sweden
^{Credits} Photography by Tomas Näsström, Jiri Adamik-Novak

—
TWOPOINTS.NET

[04]   Montjuic de Nit

Identity for an annual culture festival located on Montjuïc.

^{Client} Institut de Cultura de Barcelona

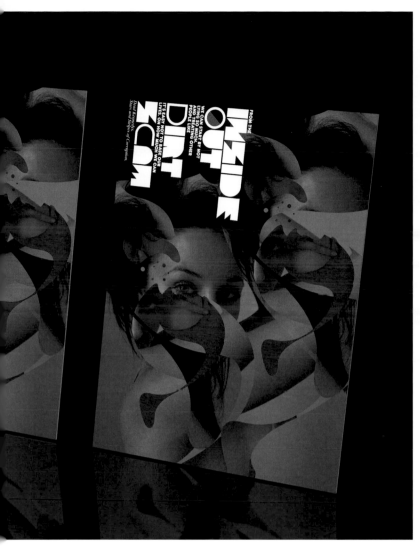

—
CLUSTA

[01] Synth Eastwood - Inside Out

Poster for the 2007 Synth Eastwood exhibition in Dublin, Ireland.

Client Synth Eastwood
Credits Photography by Martin Donnelly /
Typography by Daniel Westwood

[04] XY

Poster as part of an exploration of organic
typography focusing on the letter X and Y
for an exhibition in New York

Client Typecon Exhibition NYC

—
CLUSTA
Martin Donnelly

[02] Known As Unknown

Poster as part of a personal project exploring
typography and photography.

—
CLUSTA
Daniel Westwood Joe Micthelmore

[03] Hybrid

Light box images produced for the Plus
Design Festival 08 Exhibition in Birmingham,
United Kingdom.

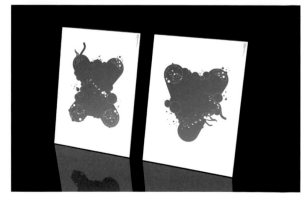

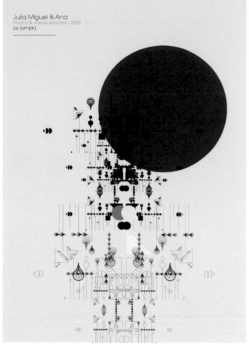

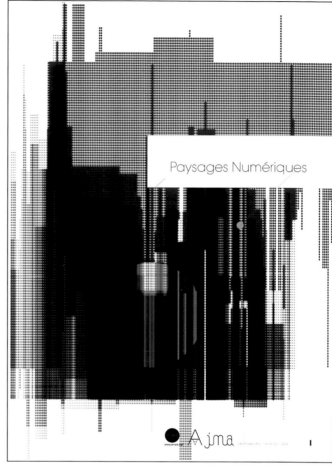

EMPK
Diego Bellorin

[01] Spacializer

CD digipak and poster.

Client Empk / Julia Miguel y Ana

[02] Paysages Numériques / audio sessions

Poster featuring a graphic interpretation
of different sounds recorded in the street
and at home. This project is the continuation
of Paysages Numeriques V.01 and is still
in progress.

Client Empk

[03] Spacializer

Poster

Client Empk / Julia Miguel y Ana

Julia Miguel & Ana
Photos & videos selection. 2008
by {empk}

112

BILLY BEN

[01] The Datsuns

Poster for a concert at Fri-Son Club.

Client Fri-Son

[02] Pravda Advert

Printed advert proposition used
in Magazines.

Client Couleur 3 – Radio Suisse Romande
Credits Creative Commons / Public Domain Images

IMJ
Jae-Hyouk Sung

[03] 2009=31536001 sec. (version 2)

Poster for self-initiated project called
Monthly Poster Series 2009.

W//:THEM / Floyd Schulze &
FAGETA / Adeline Mollard

[04–05] OPAK Magazin (Cover & Poster)

Cover and poster for a bimonthly independent magazine exploring politics,
literature, music, art and fashion under
a central theme, that will differ in
each issue.

Credits Cover Photography by Michel Bonvin /
Typeface Simplon by Emmanuel Rey

THOMAS WISMEIER

[06] Blank Space

Poster designed for Arnhemse Nieuwe,
which is a presentation of designers recently graduated from art school.

Client OPA

[01]

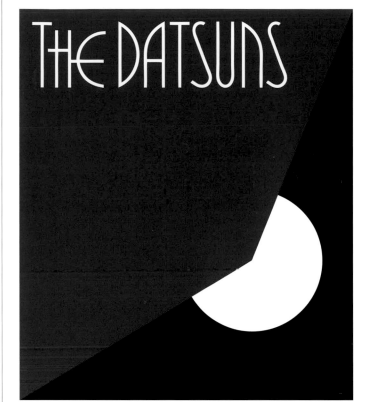

[02]

[03]

[04]

009.
15.
00.
ec.

OPAK #01

Dispo = Disco. / Release = Party.

Wir müssen releasen mit...

▶ Olsen and the Hurley Sea
[live, B], Krass + Crazy (Sinn-
ous, B], DJ Aframm [Michelle
Records, HH] und Gäste ■

AM 26.03. IM KMA36

Sei da oder sei Quadrat! Einlass: 21.ᵒᵒh

OPAK Magazin

[05]

[06]

Huub de Lang, Marius Hofstede,
Simone Trum, Saakje Visser,
Maarten van der Horst,
Lieveke van Zuylen,
Bastiaan Buurman &
Marko Matic

EXPo
Arnhemse
Nieuwe
2008

Alleen vanavond boven
in de Van Ranzowzaal!
Tijdens het programma is
de expo gesloten.

GEOPEND
~19.00 uur tot 20.00 uur.
~In de pauze.
~Na afloop van het
programma tot 24.00 uur.

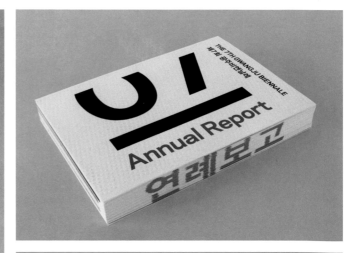

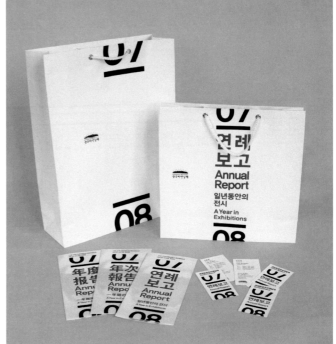

BASE DESIGN

Gwangju Biennale

Identity for The Gwangju Biennale including
catalogue, visitor guidebook, magazine ads,
press releases, stationery, signage and a
visitor map.

Client Gwangju Biennale

[02]

[03]

—
ALISTAIR WEBB & POVILAS UTOVKA

[01] Code Share Identity

Poster created for Code Share, an exhibition at the Contemporary Arts Centre, Vilnius, Lithuania. Featuring work from 20 international artists.

Client CAC Vilnius, Lithuania
Credits Photography by Thomas Manneke

[02] Umbro Future of Football

Catalogue produced for a collaborative project between Umbro and MA Fashion students at the Royal College of Art.

Client Umbro & MA Fashion at Royal College of Art, London

—
JAE-HYOUK SUNG

[03] Zero-One Spot Exhibition 2008

Exhibition poster for Zero-One Spot 2008 at the Zero-One Design Center in Seoul, Korea.

Client Zero-One Design Center

[02]

[03]
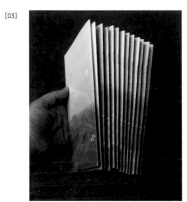

[01]

[05|06]

FRÉDÉRIC TESCHNER STUDIO

[01]   La Force de L'art

First triennial catalogue.

[02]   Seize Nouvelles Pièces Un Nouveau Lieu

Catalogue publishing Archibooks

[03–04]   Chaumont Festival

Poster and identity for the 19th international poster and graphic design festival.

[05–06]   Self Production Poster

[07]   Plein Soleil / DCA

Catalogue and invitation for the Plein Soleil / Summer of Arts centre festival.

[01|02]

[03]

ARCHITECTURE LIVE 6 'ALUMNI'

ALUMNI – NETWORKS REVISITED, 14/15 MAY 2009, AT THE UNIVERSITY OF APPLIED ARTS VIENNA, INSTITUTE OF ARCHITECTURE.
HITOSHI ABE, CECIL BALMOND, HERWIG BAUMGARTNER, ERIK BERNHARD, ALFREDO BRILLEMBOURG, IRMGARD FRANK, MARIE THERESE
HARNONCOURT, HUBERT HERMANN, BARBARA IMHOF, JEFFREY KIPNIS, HUBERT KLUMPNER, SYLVIA LAVIN, BART LOOTSMA, CAREN
ORHALING, MAX RIEDER, WOLFGANG TSCHAPELLER, THOMAS VIZKE, MICHAEL WALRAFFE, CARMEN WIEDERIN, SUSANNE ZOTTL.

XYZ.CH
Alexander Meyer

[01] Wedding Invitation

Invitation and folded poster for a wedding.

Client Berhard Meyer & Charlotte Sadowski-Crown

[02] Today Flyer

Client Besame Mucho

PAULUS M. DREIBHOLZ

[03] Architecture Live (4,5,6), limited edition

Limited edition posters for the participants of
the annual Architecture Live workshops.

Client Institute of Architecture, University of
Applied Arts Vienna
Editor Roswitha Janowski-Fritsch
Publisher IoA
Credits Screen-printed by Olivia Sautreuil

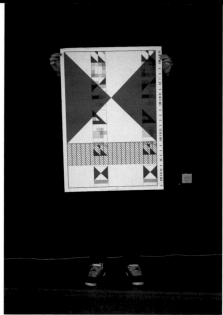

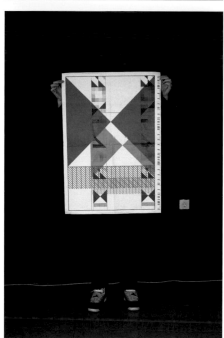

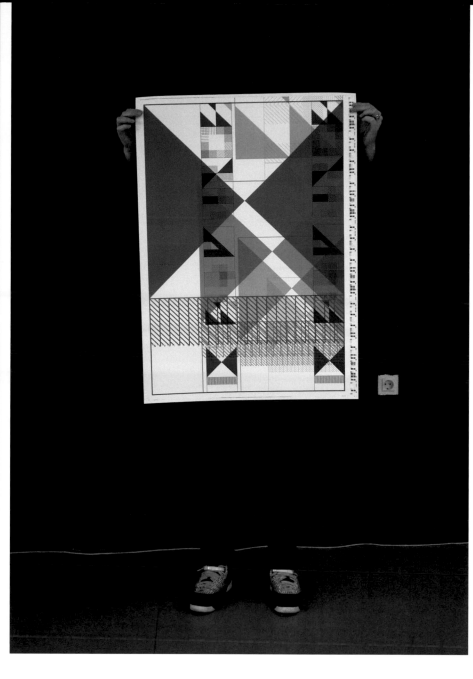

[05]

COUP
Erica Terpstra & Peter van den Hoogen

[04]   Sonic Acts XI (Printing Sheet)

Client Sonic Acts

[05]   Sonic Acts XI (CD Inlay)

Visual Identity for Sonic Acts: A Computer Art Festival.

Client Sonic Acts
Editor Arie Altena Lucas van der Velden
Publisher Sonic Acts Press, Amsterdam

[01]

[02]

[03]

JOSHUA DISTLER

[01] BY:AMT

Packaging and typeface for Alissia Melka-
Teichroew's jewelry, framing each product
with a digitally rendered image of
classical art.

Client BY:AMT
Credits With Mike Abbink

WEISS–HEITEN DESIGN
Tobias Kohlhaas, Birgit Hölzer,
Andrea Tinnes

[02] Megastructure Reloaded

Corporate, catalogue and exhibition design
for Art project.

Client European Art Projects
Editor Markus Richter and Sabrina van der Ley
Publisher Hatje Cantz

BASE DESIGN

[03] La Force de l'Art

Exhibition identity design based on three
colours. This typeface was designed especial-
ly for the exhibition.

Client Le Grand Palais

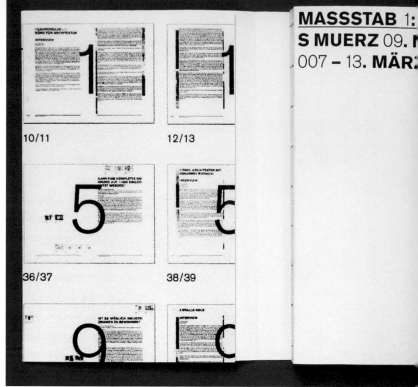

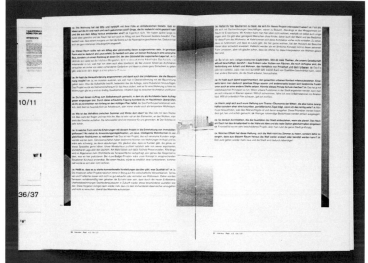

EDITORIAL DESIGN

The digital distribution of information over the Internet has led to changes in printed material. Magazines now serve as portfolios for the creative output of their editors and publishers. Magazine producers now function more like advertising agencies, and the financial viability of magazines is more dependent on 'advertorials' than on actual sales figures.

'Advertorials' are content paid for by clients, which generally refer to clients' products in a subliminal manner. This type of co-operation with clients gives fashion, lifestyle and cutting-edge magazines an opportunity to try out new, innovative graphic ideas and establish a strong identity using visual and content-based distinguishing features. The information and service sections of magazines – which used to be very detailed – have shrunk and are now only to be found on the magazines' websites. Nowadays, editorial design has other tasks to fulfil. Content is presented using more space, and articles often run over many pages and engage in 'visual storytelling'. Interrelationships within the magazine literally 'unfold' to the readers over the course of a number of pages.

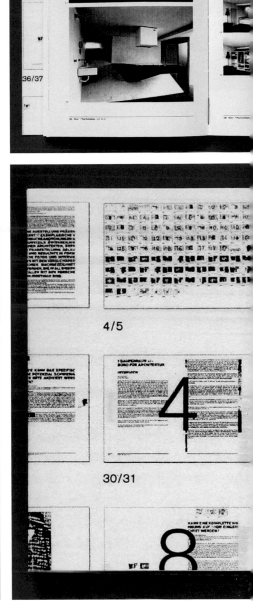

THAU
BER 2

10/11

36/37

RAUB +/– BÜRO FÜR ARCHITEKTUR WIENF
2 POOL ARCHITEKTEN TO-PENTHOUSE 3
LB VISCOSE.CH 4 DRIENDL*ARCHITECTS O
FRIEDEL WINKLER OUT OF ROSENHEIM 6
RL GRAN FIASKO 7 HERWIG SPIEGL SUCH
LZBOX MINIBOX 9 MAX RIEDER EXPERIM
HOLZHAUS 10 PPAG ARCHITECTS SH / SCH
E 11 REINHARDT HONOLD GLASHAUS 12 A
TRAUSS DASPARKHOTEL 13 ANTONIUS LA
M9 ARCHITEKTEN EINFAMILIENHAUS LAN
HELEN & HARD AS B-CAMP 15 LORENZ POT
FTÄGIGER TAGESAUSFLUG 16 ROGER BOL
& MARTIN RAUCH LEHMHAUS SCHLINS 17
ELZHAMMER MAISON TURQUOISE

SELBSTVERSUCHE BILDER

Graphic trends are developed. This includes an ex-aggerated summary of the entire contents on the covers of the publications. Similar visual trends are being developed for books and magazines, and these will eventually be adopted by mainstream media and publishers as well. All design disciplines (typography, illustration, photography) will typically be employed in the editorial design of magazines. Magazine design serves as a field for experimentation for modern graphics, as many graphic designers publicise themselves using self-produced, personal publications and magazines as a means of competing for design work in the areas of culture, advertising and lifestyle.

—
PIROL
Ruth Amstutz

Massstab 1:1 Kunsthaus Muerz
9. November 2007 – 13. März 2008

Book for an exhibition about experimental architecture. The book is structured into two parts, one containing text and the other visuals.

JONAS VOEGELI

Swiss designer Jonas Voegeli was born in Zurich in 1979 and has lived there ever since. His decision to pursue a career in graphic design was an easy choice; it is the only thing, he says rather modestly, he was ever good at. So he enrolled to study visual communication at HGKZ (Hochschule für Gestaltung und Kunst Zurich), from which he graduated in 2001 with the German equivalent of a master's degree.

Voegeli cut his professional design teeth at Basel-based studio, *MüllerHess*, where he worked for a year after graduating. From here he returned to his home-town to co-found design studio *The Remingtons* with fellow *MüllerHess* designer Ludovic Balland. Then, in 2005, Voegeli set up a studio on his own under the name *voegeli jtv*. The studio specialises in what Voegeli himself describes as 'books and brands', meaning that he works both for cultural and commercial clients, two sectors which he believes are influencing each other more and more. Clients include: the Aargauer Kunsthaus museum, the Bundesamt für Kultur/BAK, Collegium Helveticum/ETH, the Institute for Computer Music and Sound Technology/HMT Zurich, retailer Migros, the Museum für Gestaltung Zurich and Warner Music.

Not satisfied with just one studio, however, in 2009 Voegeli also set up *Hubertus*, co-founded in 2000 with art school colleagues: Philipp Schubiger, Vinzenz Blaas and Benjamin Roffler.

On the issue of his design process, Voegeli says: "I have my very own position regarding the work process in design. I think it's all about methodologies, which doesn't mean a specific use of different tools or software. It's much more about your personal condition; how you are, how you feel. You have to be in a good mood to do good stuff. This does not mean that you have to be happy to design, but you need a certain environment to act in a suitable way. Basically it's very important to find your personal position relating to the job before starting to design. But of course, all this has to do with a very personal design approach."

[01]

[02]

[03]

JONAS VOEGELI

[01–02] Saalschutz

Poster for a Swiss music band.
Client Saalschutz

[03] Grell Zahnraeder

Client Annette Grell

JONAS VOEGELI, KURT ECKERT &
MARIETTA EUGSTER

[04] Alex Hanimann, Textarbeiten

Client Aargauer Kunsthaus
Editor Stephan Kunz
Publisher Verlag für moderne Kunst Nürnberg

[04]

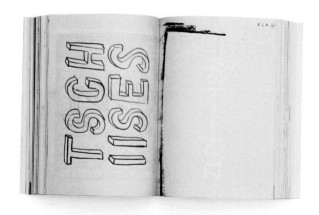

WAYNE DALY & ELEANOR DUFFIN

[01, 05] Stills From AC37

Book containing extracts from AC37,
a multi-channel video installation by artist
Eleanor Duffin.

Client / Publisher For Further Information

WAYNE DALY

[02, 06] A Glossary (With Some Pieces of Verse)

The book is a facsimile of the original
edition from 1867, an account of Yola, an
extinct Germanic language from Daly's
home county of Wexford in Ireland, spo-
ken between the 14th and 19th centuries
and thought to have been introduced by
English settlers.

Client / Publisher For Further Information
Editor Jacob Poole & Willam Barnes
Credits Page layout by Wayne Daly /
Originally typeset by R.D. Webb & Son, Dublin

[03, 04] The Names

Book containing an alphabetical register
of 20,000 spammer aliases, collected by
Daly between 2003 and 2008.

Client / Publisher For Further Information

[01]

[02]

[03]

[04]
[05]
[06]

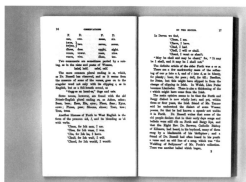
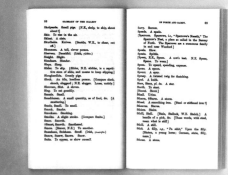

[01]

[02]

REMCO VAN BLADEL

[01] Three Ideophones

Box desgined for three 10inch vinyl records.

Publisher Onomatopee

[02] Vis à Vue

Client / Publisher Onomatopee
Editor Freek Lomme

ERIK DE HAAS & HUGO NABER

[03] Kapital K, A Classless Character

Client / Publisher Onomatopee
Editors Freek Lomme, Remco van Bladel,
Linda Aarts, Eric de Haas

TOMAS CELIZNA & DANIEL HARDING

[04] Yale University School of Art 2008 MFA
Painting & Printmaking, Sculpture

Two catalogues, produced in collaboration
with students and faculty of the Yale School
of Art addressing the limitations of print-on-
demand service.

Client / Publisher Yale University School of Art

KAPITAL K, A CLASSLESS CHARACTER

[04]

[03]

[04]

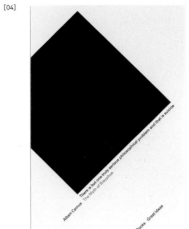

[01|02|03]

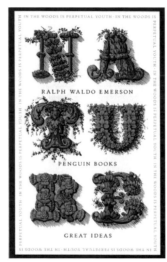

[05]

[06|07]

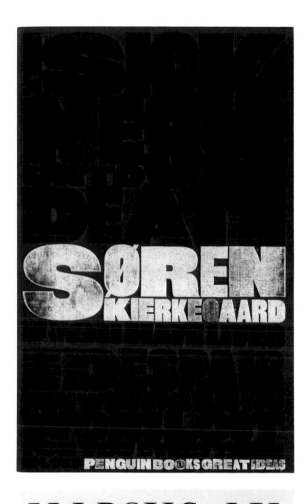

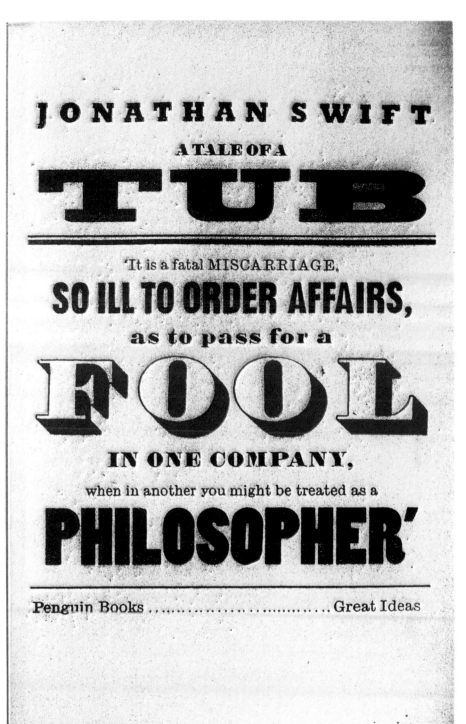

[10]

MARCUS AU
RELIUS · MED
ITATIONS · A
LITTLE FLES
H, A LITTLE
BREATH, AN
D A REASON
TO RULE AL
L — THAT IS M
YSELF · PENG
UIN BOOKS
GREAT IDEAS

[11|12|13]

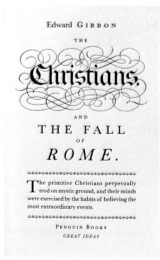

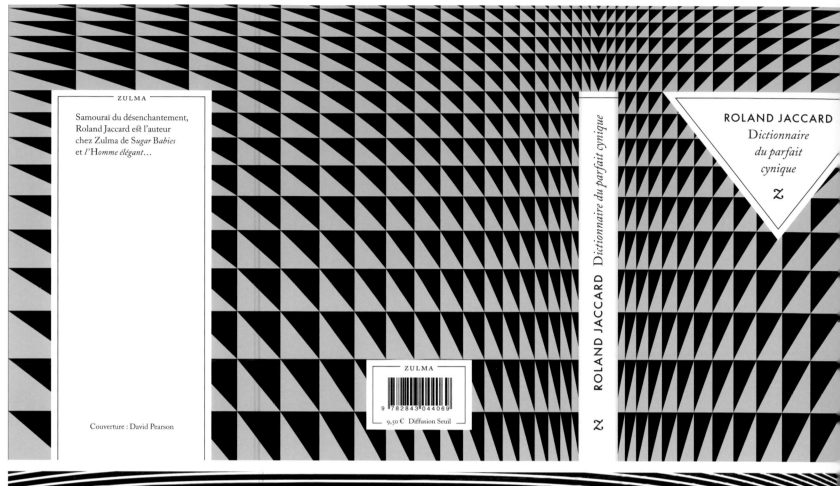

ZULMA

Samouraï du désenchantement, Roland Jaccard est l'auteur chez Zulma de *Sugar Babies* et *l'Homme élégant…*

Couverture : David Pearson

ZULMA

9,50 € Diffusion Seuil

ROLAND JACCARD *Dictionnaire du parfait cynique*

z

ROLAND JACCARD
Dictionnaire du parfait cynique

z

ZULMA

La vie de Pascal Garnier est à elle seule un roman. On retiendra qu'il est une figure originale du roman contemporain. Il a élu domicile dans un petit village de l'Ardèche où il peint, et écrit aussi des romans pour la jeunesse.

On ne s'étonnera pas qu'on lui ait donné le Grand Prix de l'Humour noir en 2006 pour *Flux*. Après *les Hauts du bas* et *l'A26*, *Comment va la douleur ?* confirme, si besoin était, son immense talent.

Couverture : David Pearson

ZULMA

16,50 € Diffusion Seuil

PASCAL GARNIER *Comment va la douleur ?*

z

PASCAL GARNIER
Comment va la douleur ?

z

ZULMA

Avec des dessins
de Roland Topor

De Sénèque à Woody Allen, en
passant par Chamfort, Wilde
ou Cioran, Roland Jaccard nous
offre ici un recueil de citations
aussi cruelles que drôles. Et pas
toujours authentiques, en parfait
cynique qu'il prétend être.
Un insolent bréviaire que
Roland Topor accompagne de
ses féroces et facétieux dessins.

www.zulma.fr

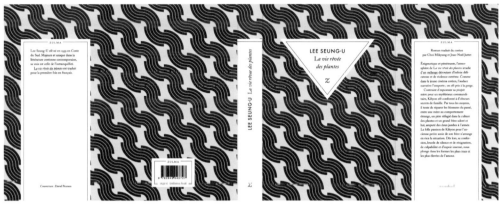

03

ZULMA

Roman

On ne saurait dire pourquoi l'univers
de Pascal Garnier nous est si proche.
Pourquoi il nous envoûte avec des his-
toires plutôt simples, des personnages
a priori ordinaires et malmenés par la
vie, des mots familiers et des silences
qui le sont encore plus.
Ainsi Bernard, crétin solaire qui
pose sur le monde un doux regard
écarquillé. C'est ce qui séduit Simon,
le cynique et élégant Simon, « éradi-
cateur de nuisibles » en préretraite,
autant dire tueur à gages au bout du
rouleau. La rencontre a lieu à Vals-
les-Bains. Et le hasard fait bien les
choses : Simon a de l'argent, et
Bernard, tout son temps. Il sera son
chauffeur pour sa dernière mission…

Avec affection, on range les romans
de Pascal Garnier au panthéon de nos
auteurs d'atmosphère. Entre Simenon
et Hardellet. Entre tendresse et
cynisme, réalisme et humour désen-
chanté. Dans *Comment va la douleur ?*
on retrouve cette façon si singulière et
si attachante qui comme un miracle
réjouit le cœur et fait du bien à l'âme.

www.zulma.fr

DAVID PEARSON

Publisher Éditions Zulma

[01]

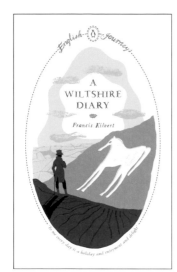 

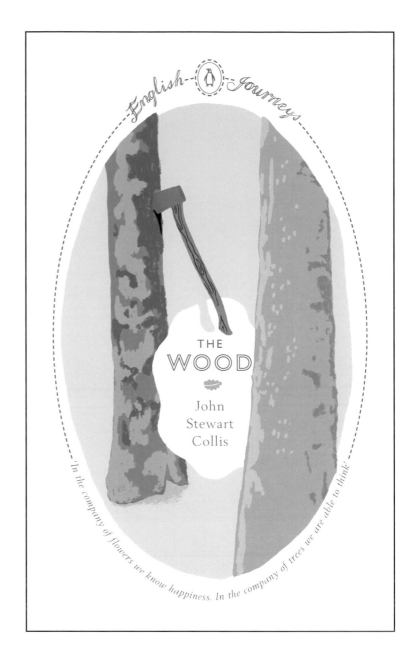

[02]

—
NATHAN BURTON
[01]   *English Journeys Cover Series*
Publisher Penguin

—
JIM STODDART & ANDY BRIDGE
[02]   Richard Feynman Cover Series
Publisher Penguin

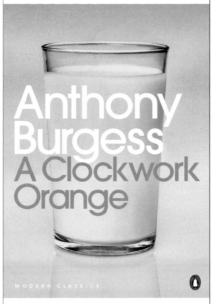

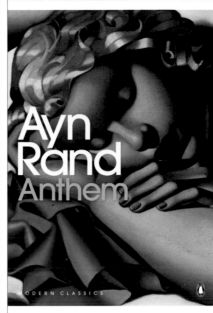

[03]

[04]

[05]

—
BASE DESIGN

IRRESPEKTIV

Art book highlighting the work of artist Kendell Geers. Geers' signature *Fuck* pattern, a key part of the artist's vocabulary, is printed across the side of the book using a proprietary software developed by BaseLab.

Client Kendell Geers
Publisher BOM

MMM

Magazine created for the communications of an opera house.

Client La Monnaie / De Munt
Credits Art Direction Pierre Daras

La Monnaie De Munt

Programs as private editions for the opera. Each opera has its own booklet with full text.

Client La Monnaie / De Munt

La Monnaie De Munt

Seasonal brochure including descriptions of the opera's performances throughout the year.

Client La Monnaie / De Munt

[01]

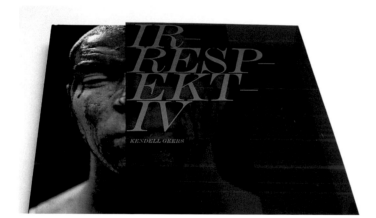

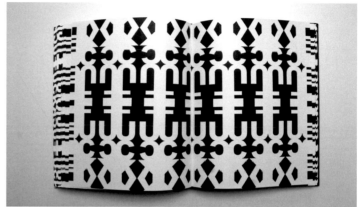

[02]

[03]

[04]

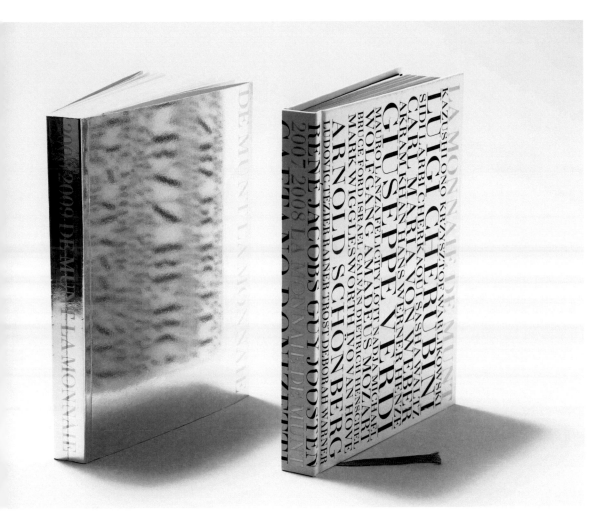

[05]

Drei. Das Triptychon in der Moderne

Richard Artschwager, Francis Bacon,
Giacomo Balla, Bill Beckley, Max Beckmann,
Joe Coleman, Jonas Dahlberg, Otto Dix,
Felix Droese, Pierre Dubreuil, Adolf Fleischmann,
Isa Genzken, Franz Gertsch, Damien Hirst,
Ellsworth Kelly, Jürgen Klauke, Yves Klein,
Oskar Kokoschka, Käthe Kollwitz, Jannis Kounellis,
Gotthardt Kuehl, Robert Longo, Markus Lüpertz,
Walter De Maria, Pia Maria Martin,
Jonathan Meese, Bjørn Melhus, Hermann Nitsch,
Oscar Obier, Sigmar Polke, Gerhard Richter,
Ricarda Roggan, Dieter Roth, Niki de Saint Phalle,
Sean Scully, Katharina Sieverding, Willi Sitte,
Hiroshi Sugimoto, Sophie Taeuber-Arp,
Antoni Tàpies, Fritz von Uhde, Emilio Vedova,
Bill Viola, Herman de Vries, Pablo Wendel

[06]

Imagine being lost in transit, stuck in an odd place together with a guy named Barry. He's more of the silent type but once he gets going, it's hard to stop her. She will speak about the future, the past and the place she is from, in ways which aren't that easy to comprehend. She talks in images, allusions and ciphers. Sometimes she gesticulates so intensely that her gestures seem like they are part of a ballet of sorts. Conversing with Barry becomes like performing some kind of choreography together. After a while there are moments when you feel you catch his drift and get his jokes. Was he even joking? With Barry it's difficult to tell. But there are some things you have in common: you both love Hitchcock and you'd do anything to leave this place behind. So you go, you travel with Barry to magical and mysterious places. Other times you just go for coffee or a walk in the park. The exact nature of your travels is difficult to describe. You might say, they feel a bit like two years at an art school and one exhibition.

[07]

—
L2M3
Ina Bauer, Sascha Lobe

[05] Drei: Das Triptychon in der Moderne

Exhibition catalogue using quotes from the
Bible as a design theme.

Client Kunstmuseum Stuttgart
Editor Marion Ackermann
Publisher Hatje Cantz, Ostfildern-Ruit

—
BASE DESIGN/ BASEWORDS

[06] Write or Wrong

Notebook as part of the identity for a
Brussels-based bookstore.
Client BozarShop
Credits Copywriting Tom Greenwood

—
SANDRA KASSENAAR

[07] Small Talk with the Janitor

Catalogue published in conjunction with the
exhibition *My Travels with Barry*.

Client / Publisher Piet Zwart Institute, Postgraduate
Studies & Research, Rotterdam, The Netherlands
Editors Anke Bangma, Ruth Buchanan,
Steve Rushton

[01]

[02]

[03]

CORINNE ZELLWEGER

P. 136 – 137

Corinne Zellweger was born in 1976 to Swiss parents in Tehran, Iran. Her family returned to Lucerne in Switzerland shortly afterwards and this is where Zellweger grew up. Between 1999 and 2004, she studied graphic design at ESAG (École Supérieure d'Arts Graphiques) Penninghen, which included a year's study at Konstfack University College of Arts, Crafts and Design in Stockholm, Sweden as part of an Erasmus exchange.

After graduating with her MA in 2004, Zellweger enjoyed a brief design internship with design studio *M/M* in Paris, before moving to Zurich in Switzerland, where she secured her first job as a designer for *Studio Cornel Windlin*. From here, Zellweger worked for herself, returning to live in both Stockholm in 2006 and Lucerne in 2007, where she set up her design studio, before finally moving in 2008 to Geneva, where she lives today.

Working mainly in printed matter and with a focus on magazine and book design, Zellweger's work also includes logotypes, identities, flyers, posters and the occasional website. Cultural clients to date include Centre Pompidou Paris, ICS (Institute for Cultural Studies in the Arts) Zurich, MUDAC (Musée de Design et d'Arts Appliqué Contemporain) in Lausanne and the Tate Gallery, London. Zellweger collaborates with other graphic designers regularly. In the past, these have included Kristina Brusa, Gavillet & Rust, Rafael Koch and Urs Lehni.

Though she has many inspirations, on the day of interview Zellweger cited Danish silversmith and wooden toy designer, Kay Bojesen (1886–1958).

CORINNE ZELLWEGER

[01] Harald Szeemann – Individual Methodology

Book designed to refer to Szeemanns archive on which the research was based.

Client Le Magasin – Centre National d'Art Contemporain de Grenoble, in collaboration with the Department of Curating Contemporary Art, Royal College of Art, London
Editor Florence Derieux
Publisher JRP|Ringier

CORINNE ZELLWEGER & MARTIN FROSTNER

[02] Mars 06

Newsletter and booklet design for Färgfabriken including the photography of Armin Linke, whose work was being exhibited.

Client Färgfabriken – Center for Contemporary Art and Architecture, Stockholm
Editor Jan Aman
Publisher Färgfabriken – Center for Contemporary Art and Architecture, Stockholm

CORINNE ZELLWEGER GAVILLET & RUST

[03] Voids – A Retrospective

Book featuring a catalogue section that documents a selected historical and contemporary exhibitions. The publication also contains an anthology of more than forty texts, as well as contributions by artists.

Client Centre Pompidou, Centre Pompidou-Metz, Kunsthalle Bern
Editors John Armleder, Mathieu Copeland, Laurent Le Bon, Gustav Metzger, Mai-Thu Perret, Clive Phillpot, Philippe Pirotte
Publisher JRP|Ringier Zürich

CORINNE ZELLWEGER & URS LEHNI

[04] The Locations – Margot Zanni

Book monograph about Zurich-based artist Margot Zanni, showing 9 of her works.

Client / Editor Margot Zanni
Publisher Edition Fink Zürich

[04]

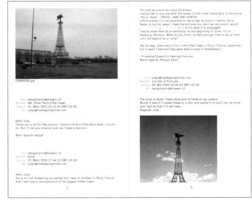

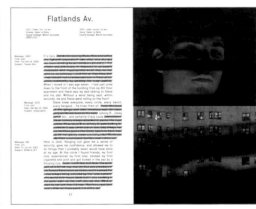

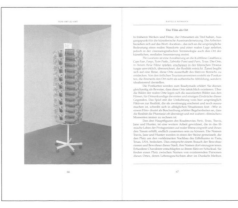

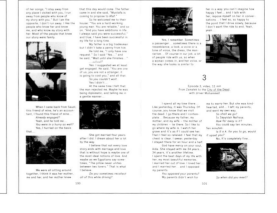

PROJEKTTRIANGLE DESIGN STUDIO

[01] Holzmedia Look book 2.0

Editorial Design and photography for
a media furniture manufacturer.

Client / Publisher Holzmedia GmbH

[02] Hollin + Radoske Architects

Corporate Design including office stationery and special mailings for Franfurt-based
architects.

Client Hollin + Radoske Architects
Material / Print Technique Hot Foil Stamping, Embossing,
Offset Printing

[02]

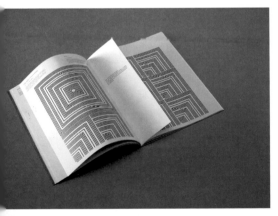

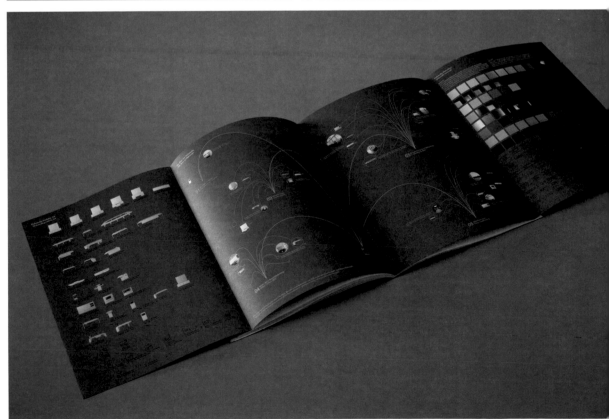

[01]

—
ONLAB
Nicolas Bourquin

[01] Design Reaktor Berlin

Book consisting of 5 books binded within a
leporello, documenting the experimental
projects on product design that unite students of the university, business executives
and market needs. Each booklet has an
independent layout.

Client / Publisher Berlin University of the Arts (UdK)
Editors Design Reaktor Berlin: Prof. Axel Kufus,
Judith Seng, Marc Piesbergen,
Joachim Schirrmacher
Credits Concept, art direction, design by onlab,
Nicolas Bourquin, Sven Ehmann, Yassin Baggar,
Marte Meling Enoksen, Matthias Hübner,
Sueh Li Tan, Thibaud Tissot, Kasper Zwaaneveld /
Management by Rainalt Jossé, Judith Wimmer /
Cover picture (inner page) by Paul Graves

[02] Updating Germany –

100 projects for a better future

Exhibition catalogue of the German contribution to the 11th International Architecture Exhibition at the Venice Biennale 2008
featuring one hundred architecture, art, and
design projects.

Client Raumtaktik
Editor Raumtaktik, Friedrich von Borries,
Matthias Böttger
Publisher Hatje Cantz
Credits Art Direction by onlab, Nicolas Bourquin /
Design, layout by onlab, Linda Hintz, Matthias
Hübner / Cover image by Jan Bruehhel the
Younger, Paradise, 1640–1660

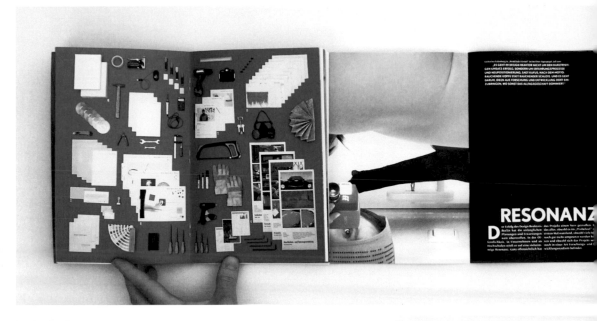

RESONANZ

PRAXIS UND EXPERIMENT

SCHRITTE IN DEN MARKT

POTENZIALE

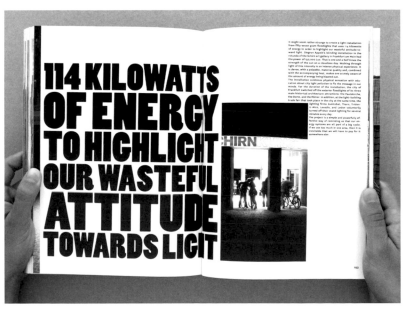

100 PROJECTS FOR A BETTER FUTURE

UPDATING GERMANY

114 KILOWATTS OF ENERGY TO HIGHLIGHT OUR WASTEFUL ATTITUDE TOWARDS LIGHT

Marie Lusa was born in Jura, Switzerland in 1976. It was at the age of 11 that Lusa decided she wanted to be a graphic designer because, as she puts it: "I thought that so many things around looked so sad."

Trained in graphic design at the University of Art and Design (ECAL), Lausanne, Lusa graduated in 2000, before moving to Zurich to set up her own studio in early 2001. Lusa has been helping the world look happier ever since.

Lusa designs, illustrates and photographs for a list of clients which spans art institutions, artists, writers, curators, philosophers, watchmakers, publishing houses and advertising agencies. Though she finds collaborations with artists perhaps most interesting, her favourite project to date has been creating the publicity for the 2009 exhibition *Giacometti, Balthus, Skira – Les Annees Labyrinthe*, at Zurich-based *Migros Museum Fur Gegenwartskunst*. To promote the exhibition on the 1940s surrealist magazine *Labyrinthe*, Lusa created five different newspapers featuring excerpts from the periodical. The art direction and concept was developed in collaboration with the exhibition's curator, Stefan Zweifel.

Inspired by colours, Lusa cites "alpine rose, insolent grey, drab brown, Verona brown, deep pool blue, papaya gold, true cinnamon and wild lavender" as being amongst her favourites.

DERRIERE LA COLLINE
Marie Lusa

[01–02] Giacometti, Balthus, Skira Les années
Labyrinthe (1944–1946)

Journal addressing surrealism, eroticism
in the context of magazines of the 1930s
as well as debating existentialism.

Client / Publisher Musée d'art et d'histoire Genève
Editor Stefan Zweifel

[03] Collection / Sammlung

Colour Research
Client Migros Museum für
Gegenwartskunst Zürich
Editor Heike Munder
Publisher JRP Ringier Zurich

[04] Work 2004–2009

[01]

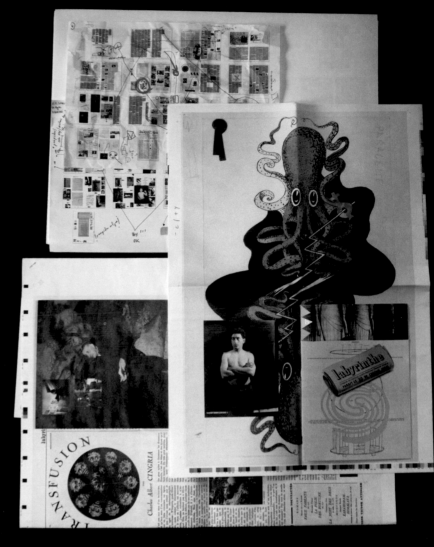

[02]

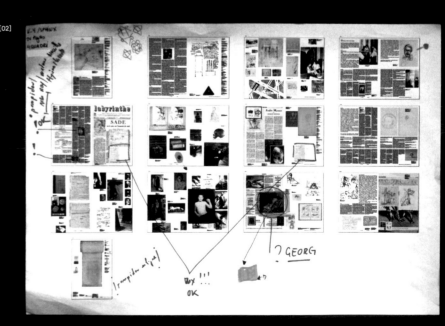

[03]

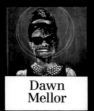

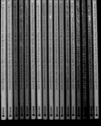

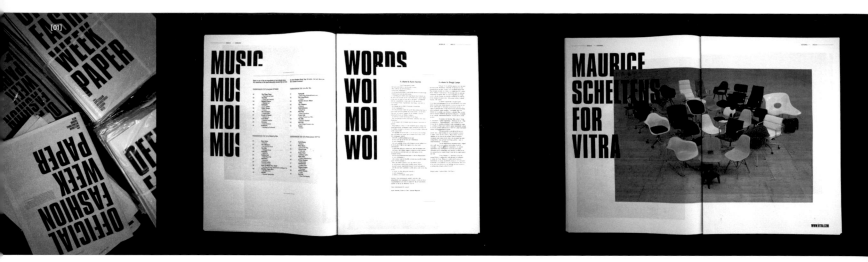

[01]

[02]

[03]

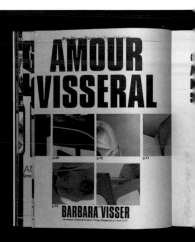

—
JULIAN BITTINER

[01] Acts of Graphic Design

MFA thesis book documenting all work
produced over the course of two years in
the graduate program at the Yale School
of Art.

Client Yale School of Art
Editor Julian Bittiner, Elizabeth Sledge, Susan
Sellers

—
HEY HO

[02–03] Collectif

Client / Publisher Arc en rêve

[01]

[02]

[01]

[02]

JUNG
UNDWENIG
P. 57, 67, 148–149

Christopher Jung was born in Pforzheim, Germany in 1975. Tobias Wenig was born in Tuebingen, also in Germany, in 1976. Together they form the design studio *jungundwenig*, which translates into English as "young and little."

Jung and Wenig first met in 1999 whilst taking the entrance exam for admission to the Hochschule Fuer Grafik und Buchkunst (Academy of Visual Arts) in Leipzig. They both succeeded and started their studies at the academy in 2000 where they were taught by, they say "outstanding teachers": these included none other than Daniela Haufe and Detlef Fiedler of studio Cyan who taught their "system design and foundation studies" course, and Günter Karl Bose who taught typography. Though they graduated in 2007, the duo started working as *jungundwenig* as early as 2004.

Working largely for the cultural sector, clients include the Goethe Institute, Berlin; Union Gallery, London; Human Rights Watch, Berlin and in Leipzig:

Museum der bildenden Künste; Galerie Kleindienst and the Red Stripe Gallery. Personal projects are, however, also very important to *jungundwenig* and they recently bought a Risograph GR 3770, a self-contained reprographics system which they describe as "a kind of silk-screen photocopying apparatus". They have finished their first book project which they say we'll get to see soon.

While Wenig cites as his inspiration, "my sons, my wife and good food," Jung's list is somewhat longer. His inspirations include, in no particular order: Paul Rand, Harmonie Corinne, skateboarding, Johann Sebastian Bach, Wassily Kandinsky, Josef Müller-Brockmann, Aphex Twin, Wolfgang Weingart, David Lynch, the Cohen brothers, Ludovic Balland, *The Simpsons*, Ren & Stimpy, Squarepusher, Bjork, Michel Gondry, DJ Koze and Mogwai.

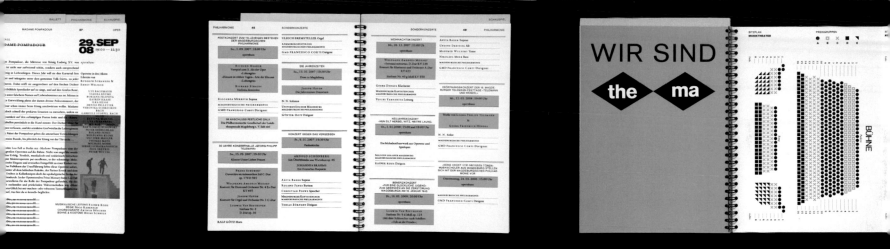

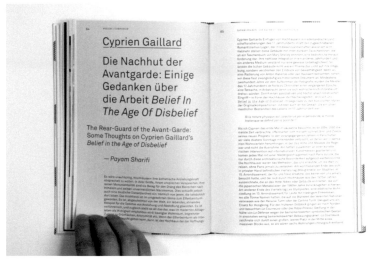

JUNG UND WENIG
Christopher Jung & Tobias Wenig

[01] Overcoming Dictatorships

Catalogue for an exhibition about the overcoming of dictatorships.

Client / Publisher Kerber Publishers
Editor Dr. Jutta Vincent

[02] Jahresprogramm für das Theater Magdeburg

Client Theater Magdeburg
Credits Photography by Nikolaus Brade

JUNG UND WENIG
Christopher Jung,
Tobias Wenig & Pascal Storz

[03] FUSION // CONFUSION

Book about contemporary art.

Client Folkwang Museum
Editor Dr. Sabine Maria Schmidt
Publisher Verlag für Moderne Kunst Nürnberg

[01]

[02]

[03]

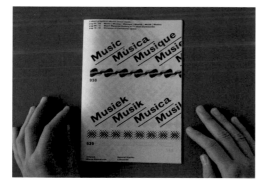

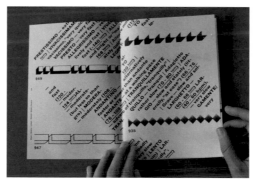

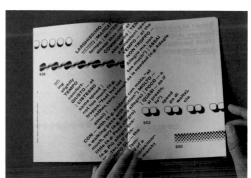

JONAS WILLIAMSSON &
MARTIN FROSTNER

[01] Forms of Inquiry / Lapis Forum on Design
and Critical Practice

Poster and leaflet for the exhibition *Forms
of Inquiry: The Architecture of Critical
Graphic Design*.

Client Laspis (The Swedish Arts Grants Commitee's
International Programme for Visual Artists)
Editor Magnus Ericsson / Laspis
Credits Curation by Zak Kyes / Architectural Association.

VELINA STOYKOVA

[02] Commissioned works / Emily Tepper

Portfolio book of the holographer
Emily Tepper.

Client / Editor Emily Tepper

LETRA
Marco Balesteros

[03] Music / Música / Musique / Musiek / Musik

Magazine contribution for the *Umool Umool*
magazine. In this project the objective was
to deal with typography, the Letraset®
elements as well as classical rhythm notions,
addressing the idea to create *Typographical Music*.

Client Umool Umool vol.8
Editor / Publisher Na Kim

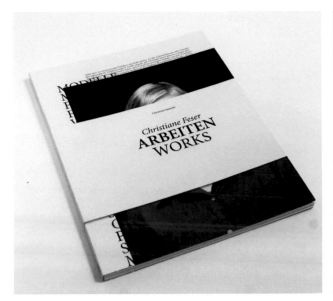

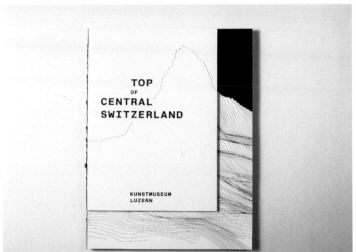

—
HI
Megi Zumstein & Claudio Barandun

[04] Top of Central Switzerland

Catalogue of the Exhibition *Top of Central Switzerland* at the Museum of Art Lucerne

Client / Publisher Kunstmuseum Luzern
Editor Peter Fischer, Christoph Lichtin, Susanne Neubauer

—
PIXELGARTEN

[05] Christiane Feser – Arbeiten / Works

Publication for the German artist Christiane Feser.

Client Christiane Feser
Publisher Verlag für moderne Kunst Nürnberg

—
ALISTAIR WEBB & EVA KELLENBERGER

[06] Arc 13

Occasional publication exploring the idea of a misconception from numerous points of view including: typeface design, commissioned writing, illustration and photography.

Editor Chloë King
Publisher Royal College of Art, London.
Credits Headline typeface by Povilas Utovka

—
ALISTAIR WEBB

[07] While The Things Of The World Still Do Not Move

A catalogue of work created by artist and illustrator Anne Harild.

[01]

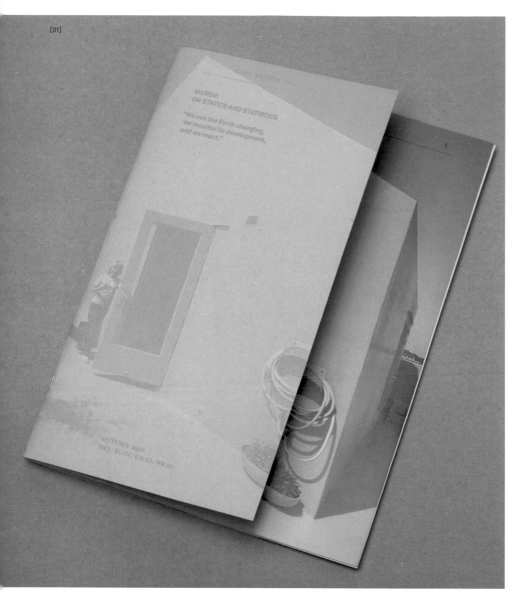

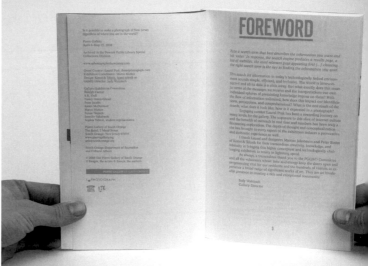

KONST
& TEKNIK

P. 41, 152 – 153

Swedish design duo *Konst & Teknik* are Mattias Jakobsson and Peter Ström. Jakobsson was born in Kalmar, Sweden in 1979 while Ström was born one year earlier in 1978 in Umeå, also in Sweden.

A truly modern partnership, they first met in 1997 on an online forum discussing the beauty of Hans Reichel's typeface, Barmeno. They set up the *Konst & Teknik* studio in Stockholm some nine years later, after graduating in 2006; Jakobsson from Beckmans College of Design in Stockholm, Ström from the Gerrit Rietveld Academy in Amsterdam.

Konst & Teknik tend to work on self-initiated as well as cultural projects for artists, curators, publishers and various institutions. Recently these include art, architecture, cinema, and the philosophy magazine, *Site*; Berlin-based art and culture magazine *Mono-Kultur*; Pierro Gallery in South Orange, New Jersey and Swedish publishing house AXL Books.

Among their self-initiated projects is the curation of a 2007 exhibition at Sandvikens Konsthall on the foundations of decision-making in graphic design and, more recently in 2008, the creation of a publication entitled *Trace a Face*, in collaboration with Amsterdam-based designer Jonathan Puckey. The publication aims to encourage and discuss the development and usage of modern tools in contemporary graphic design practice. It was released in connection with a lecture given by Jonathan Puckey in Stockholm, November 2008, and is the first in an ongoing series of collaborative publications initiated by *Konst & Teknik*.

They say they are inspired by "things we almost understand".

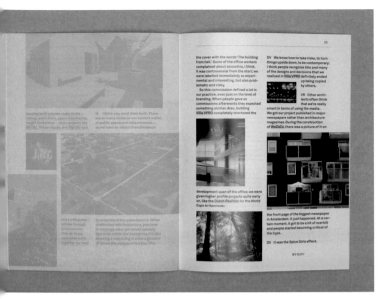

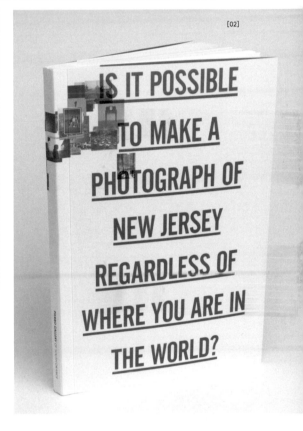

IS IT POSSIBLE TO MAKE A PHOTOGRAPH OF NEW JERSEY REGARDLESS OF WHERE YOU ARE IN THE WORLD?

[02]

[03]

—
KONST & TEKNIK

[01]   MonoKultur #18

Magazine issue featuring two interviews with Dutch experimental architects MVRDV – one with visionary theorist Winy Maas, and one with Jacob van Rijs and Nathalie de Vries. Both interviews run parallel throughout the magazine but differ in terms of paper and printing based on the character of each talk.

Client / Publisher MonoKultur
Editor Kai von Rabenau

[02]   Is it possible to make a photo of New Jersey regardless of where you are in the world?

Catalogue for an exhibition raising questions on how the internet and globalization has changed the idea of place.

Client I heart photograph / Pierro Gallery New Jersey
Editor Laurel Ptak
Publisher Pierro Gallery New Jersey

[03]   SITE Magazine

Magazine for contemporary art, architecture, cinema, and philosophy launched in 2001.

Client / Publisher SITE Magazine
Editor Sven-Olov Wallenstein

—
PRACTISE, LONDON
James Goggin & Régis Tosetti

Dominique Gonzalez-Foerster TH.2058

Catalogue and typeface for Dominique Gonzalez-Foerster's *TH.2058* installation in *Tate*.

Publisher Tate publishing
Credits Cover by Syd Mead *Rainy Expressway* (detail) 1968

RÉGIS TOSETTI

L'Art de la Chasse (The Art of Hunting)

Arist's book located somewhere between ethnographic investigation, photo-novel, and initiation epic.

Publisher JRP|Ringier, Zürich

[01]

[02|03]

BUREAU MARIO LOMBARDO
Mario Lombardo

[01] Liebling Newspaper

Client Liebling
Credits Design by Kirstin Weppner, Catrin Sonnabend, Markus Mrugalla

[02] Gute Aussichten

Client Gute Aussichten
Credits Design by Markus Mrugalla & Catrin
Sonnabend / Photography by Gute Aussichten

[03] Vertrautes Terrain

Client ZKM
Credits Design by Tania Parovic, Christian Schneider

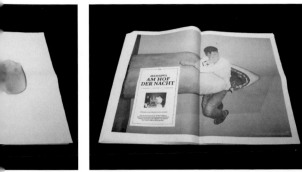
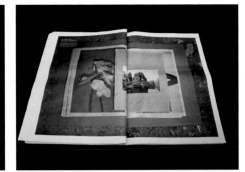

MARIO LOMBARDO

P. 156 – 159, 251

Originally from Argentina, Mario Lombardo was born in Rosario, about 300 km north of Buenos Aires near the Parana. His family relocated to Germany in 1978 because of the military junta and today Lombardo is based in Berlin, where he and his family finally settled in 2008 after stints in several of Germany's big cities.

Lombardo worked professionally both before and throughout his studies at design school, FH (Fachbereich Design) in Aachen, from which he graduated with a degree in visual communication in 2001. Projects were mostly for editorial clients and record labels and as early as 1997, Lombardo was given free rein designing the layout of the Aachen city newspaper *Klenkes*. Bureau Mario Lombardo was founded in 2004 in Cologne during the five-and-a-half year period over which Lombardo worked as art director for *SPEX* magazine.

Of his working space, Lombardo explains: "When we moved to Berlin I merged office and home. We live on two big floors, connected by a spiral staircase, the lower being the office and the upper being our apartment. My daughter, Mila, can come down whenever she likes to see us or play in our courtyard full of plants and trees." Lombardo created the office furniture using blackboards, for Mila and her friends to draw on whenever they like. "The look of our furniture is thus constantly changing," he says, "depending on the mood of the kids."

Six people work in the studio today, each focusing on a different field from editorial, video, TV, book design, and graphics to copy editing and conception. Clients include Audi, Fiat, the Goethe Institute, musician Scott Matthews, *Liebling Magazine* and Gestalten. Editorial and music design, however, remain Lombardo's favourites.

"I like to combine analogue and digital media," he explains. "On a formal level I always seek to combine a 'wow' attractor with an emotional effect. I like to create images that attract at first glance and only reveal their meta levels slowly and successively afterwards."

[01]

[02]

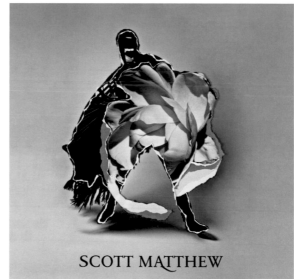

[03]

ANDREAS BUNTE

17. JANUAR – 08. MÄRZ 2009

BIELEFELDER KUNS

im Waldhof
Welle 61
D-33602 Bielefeld
bielefelder-kunstverein.de

ÖFFNUNGZEITEN
Do, Fr, 15–19 Uhr
Sa, So, 12–19 Uhr
Mo–Mi, nach telefonischer
Vereinbarung

17. JANUAR – 08. MÄRZ 2009

—
BUREAU MARIO LOMBARDO
Mario Lombardo

[01] <u>Scott Matthew</u>

Client Scott Matthew
Credits Photography by Michael Mann

[02] <u>Bielefelder Kunstverein</u>

Credits Design by Kirstin Weppner / Illustration
by Markus Mrugalla

[03] <u>The Strange Saga Of Hiroshi
The Freeloading Sex Machine</u>

Client Rapid Eye Movies

[04] <u>Michael Mann</u>

Client Michael Mann
Credits Photography by Michael Mann

[05] <u>Recréation</u>

Client Defrance
Credits Photography by Mareike Foecking

[04]

[05]

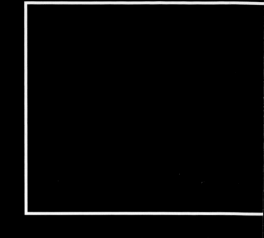

SIMONA BRÜHLMEIER

[01] Dazwischen – "noch nicht" und "nicht mehr"

Diploma Thesis at University of Arts in Bern, addressing transitional periods.

KAI-TING LIN

[02] Psycho 1960 1998

Simultaneous screening and booklet about the remake of the movie *Psycho*. The juxta-position of the two provides a visual experi-ence, synthesizing the original and the remake.

HANNES GLOOR & STEFAN JANDL

[03] Well Ko Med

Identity for a newly-founded medicine centre based in Zurich. Including logo, business card, flyer and website.

Client Well Ko Med

[02]

[01]

Il Buono
Il Brutto
&
Il Cattivo

Once upon a time
you **dressed** so fine

You threw the **bums**
a *dime* in your prime,
didn't you?

[02]

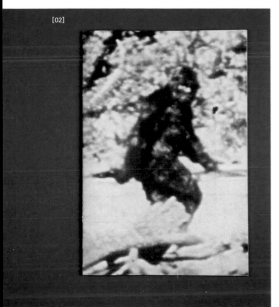

BieMen
stersch
undlich
Bewee Ve
isetter
n

Sie sind von
der Wissenschaft
bisher nicht
offiziell anerkannt,
tragen aber
zum Teil Namen,
etwa Yeti oder
Sasquatch.

Als erster echter
Mensch gilt
der Homo Habilis.

Wasund
für ewie s
in häehr
sslicähne
hes Tlt e
ier dr un
er As
ffe,

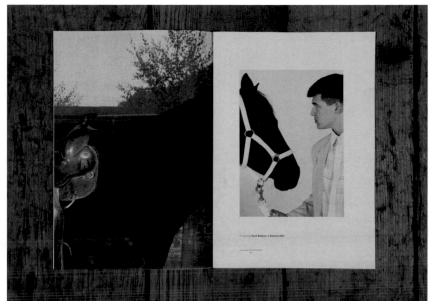

STUDIO SPORT
Ronnie Fueglister & Martin Stoecklin

[01] Il Buono, il Brutto & il Cattivo

Lookbook and poster of fashion designer
Sebastian Schibler.

Client / Publisher Sebastian Schibler
Editors Sebastian Schibler, Gina Folly, Studio Sport
Credits Photography by Gina Folly.

STUDIO SPORT
Martin Stoecklin

[02] Biester und Beweise

Book on study and search for animals which
fall outside of contemporary zoological
catalogues featuring the myths and proofs
of Bigfoot, Yeti and the like. A custom-
made hybrid typeface in two cuts was used
throughout the publication.

[01]

RAFFINIERIE AG FÜR GESTALTUNG

P. 62 – 63, 164 – 165, 191

Team Raffinerie, AG für Gestaltung is based in Zurich, Switzerland, though its 12 members hail from Switzerland, Croatia and Germany.

It was founded in 2000 by Reto Ehrbar, Nenad Kovačić and Donovan Gregory, who met at school, though Gregory has since moved on to new pastures.

Team Raffinerie design books on art and architecture and create magazine design and illustration for a range of clients including Swiss International Air Lines; the publishing house GTA Verlag; art dealer The Daros Collection; Kinki Magazine; the Swiss Arts Council, Pro Helvetia and Zurich theatres: Schauspielhaus (The Playhouse), Theaterhaus Gessnerallee and Burgtheater Wien.

Enjoying authorship as often as possible when clients are sufficiently open-minded, the studio also works on personal art projects. Most recently they have completed an illustrated fairytale entitled *Tiru* which consists of a fantastically ambitious 5.4 metre-long silkscreen 'leporello' or concertina-folding book. Other art projects include a paper laser-cut of Karl Marx and a giant portrait of four artists constructed from layers of laser-cut Plexiglas, one artist per layer.

Though they cite Swiss graphic design history as a major inspiration, they are quick to add that they are inspired by many things in everyday life that have nothing at all to do with design. Their dream project? Drawing turtles in the Maldives.

Team Raffinerie, AG für Gestaltung are: Anita Alleman, Marion Bernegger, Reto Ehrbar, Simon Fuhrimann, Christian Haas, Claire Hulla, Adrian Goepel, Nenad Kovačić, Marcus Kraft, Florian Streit, Helen Pombo, Antonia Huber.

—
RAFFINERIE AG FÜR GESTALTUNG

[01] Schauspielhaus Zürich Saison Vorschau

Credits In collaboration with Studio Achermann Zurich, Photography by Tonk

[02] Schauspielhaus Zürich Posters

Credits Photography by Patrick Hari & Cat Tuong Nguyen in collaboration with Studio Achermann Zürich

[03]

[04]

—
RAFFINERIE AG FÜR GESTALTUNG

[03] Gessnerallee Programmhefte

Client Theaterhaus Gessnerallee Zürich
Credits Photography by Hans-Jörg Walter

[04] Gessnerallee Programmhefte

Client Theaterhaus Gessnerallee Zurich
Credits Photography by Hans-Jörg Walter

[02]

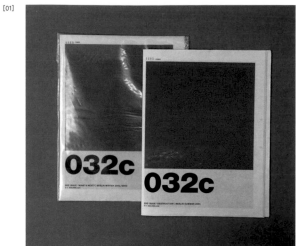

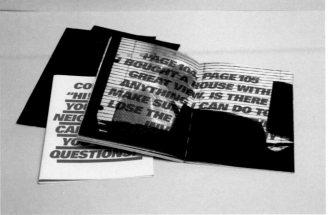

—
NODE BERLIN OSLO
Vladimir Llovet

[01] **032c**

Bi-annual contemporary culture magazine at the intersection of fashion, art and politics with a layout based purely on typography.

Client 032c Workshop/Jörg Koch

—
NODE BERLIN OSLO

[02] **Høvikodden LIVE**

Book for the Henie Onstad Art Centre's annual arena for interdisciplinary activities.

Client / Publisher Henie Onstad Art Centre, Oslo
Credits Illustrations by PenJet project

[03] **Visual Reader Ijmuiden**

A visual reader containing hundreds of photos relating to the Dutch fortress island Ijmuiden, occupied by the Germans during WW2.

[04] **Justine Frank Roee Rosen Sweet Sweat**

Book design from *Sweet Sweat*, a novel by Belgian artist Justine Frank.

Editor Hila Peleg
Client / Publisher Sternberg Press & Extra City

[05] **Minsk Urban Diary**

Catalogue and postcards for an exhibition.

Client Laznia Centre for Contemporary Art, Gdansk

[06] **Neighbours**

Book about neighbour relations realised by students from the Gerrit Rietveld Academy in Amsterdam.

Client Loyens & Loeff

[07] **KOLDING A-Z, Workshop**

Research about the city's identity, combining found footage and student projects material.

Editor Master students at Kolding Designskolen, Denmark

[08] **Heitere Weitere Polterei**

Posters and an artist monograph.

Client Galeria Toni Tàpies, Barcelona
Publisher FNAC Bourgogne

GLASHAUS

P. 61, 168 – 169

Gregor Huber and Ivan Sterzinger are *Glashaus*. The duo was born in Zurich, in 1978 and 1977 respectively, though it was not until 1996 that they first met. Both lovers of music, a chance meeting in a record shop in their native city marked the beginning of their friendship and professional relationship.

First setting up a bar-cum-gallery, *Mikro*, in the late nineties, Huber and Sterzinger then launched their design studio in the basement of the same building in 1999. This was before they had even completed their studies. While Hubert graduated with a master's degree in Media Arts from HGKZ (University of Art and Design), Zurich, Sterzinger graduated, also with a master's, though in Psychology, Media and History of Art, two years later from the University of Zurich.

Working both in print and for the web, for themselves and others, *Glashaus'* commissioned projects to date include the redesign and art direction of Zurich-based cultural institution *Rote Fabrik*'s newspaper *Fabrikzeitung*, which delivers a monthly discourse on culture, art and politics. They have also created catalogues for galleries including the *Haus für Kunst Uri*, in Altdorf, Switzerland and websites for artists including Irish-born Michael John Whelan.

Personal projects have always played an important part in *Glashaus*, explains Sterzinger: "Our latest project, Raphistory, was concerned with the proliferation and perception of rap music. In a monthly event we delivered, together with Clemens Wempe, a set of information about the history of rap music. Each set consisted of a fanzine, a mixtape, a stream and a party. The series is currently running in Berlin, and other cities are in discussion."

Sterzinger, who cites friends as his main inspiration, is currently based in London, UK for a six-month period after winning a grant from the Swiss Federal Office of Culture. Huber is inspired, he says, by "disco".

GLASHAUS
Gregor Huber & Ivan Sterzinger

[01]   Politik – Issue

[02]   Hobbytopia – Issue

[03]   Gewalt – Issue

[04]   Die Alternative – Issue

[05]   Focused on you and your Needs – Issue

[06]   On the Road (again)

Newspaper for the culture centre Rote Fabrik questions positions and representations of contemporary alternative culture.

Client Rote Fabrik
Credits Photography by Nelly Rodriguez [02]
and by Nguyen-Hari [03]

[01]

[02]

[03]

Gewalt & Medien
Die Zeitung der Roten Fabrik Januar 2009

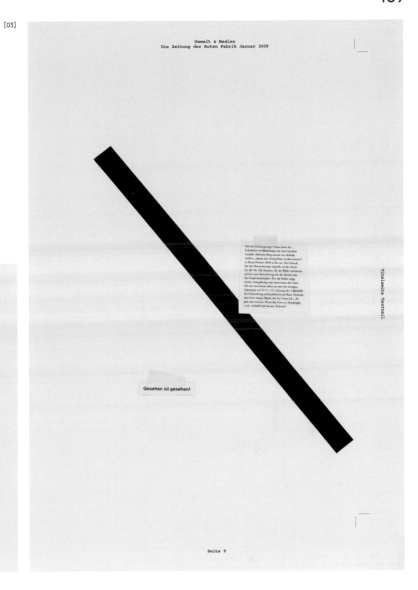

Gesehen ist gesehen!

Titelseite Textteil

Seite 9

[04]

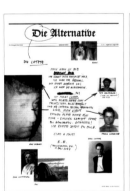

Die Alternative

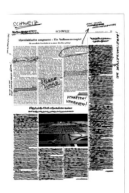

SCHWEIZ

[05]

FOCUSED
ON YOU
AND
YOUR
NEEDS

Werben bis zu Sieg

WE LIKE TO ENTER-TAIN YOU	WE WANT YOUR ADVISORY	SIE SIND UNSER GAST	YOUR FIRST SHOPPING DESTINA-TION
PLANEN SIE IHRE ZUKUNFT?	ALWAYS A SMILE	JEDEM SEIN HEIM	DAMIT KOMMEN SIE GUT AN
NEUE PER-SPEKTIVEN FÜR SIE	NÄHER BEI DEN STARS	FOCUSED ON YOU AND YOUR NEEDS	SCHÖN WENN MAN DIE WAHL HAT
NEUGKEI-TEN AUS DEM JENSEITS	BLEIB COOL MAN	EINFACH UN WIDER-STEHLICH	ER-REICHEN SIE HÖHERE ZIELE
ZWEI JAHRE DIE MICH WEITER-BRINGEN	SIE STEHEN IM MITTEL-PUNKT	WILLKOM-MEN IM WUNSCH PARADIES	FÜR BEIDE SEITEN EIN GEWINN

fabrik

[06]

ON THE ROAD
(AGAIN)

[01]

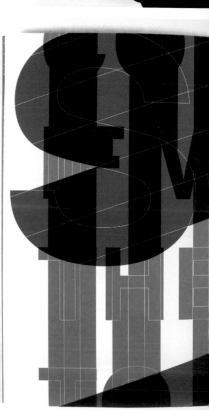

GDLOFT

[01] Philadelphia Design Awards (PDA)
Call for Entries Mailer

Brochure for the *Philadelphia Design Awards*.
As a metaphor for building community, the
brochure can be desconstructed, and pieced
together to reveal a poster.

Client American Institute of Graphic Arts, Philadelphia
Editors Allan Espiritu, Michele Cooper
Credits Art direction by Allan Espiritu / Design by
Allan Espiritu, Christian Mortlock, Sung Park

[02] Lantern Theater 15th Season Brochure

The brochure and posters utilize collage to
express an assemblage of different ideas,
influences, and people.

Client Lantern Theater Company, Philadelphia, PA
Editor Leigh Goldenberg

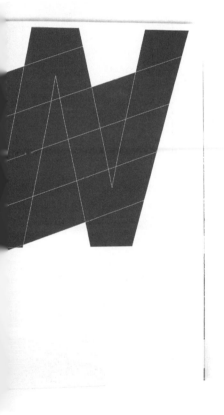

[02]

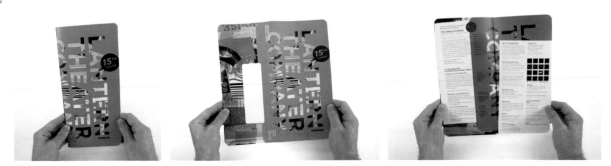

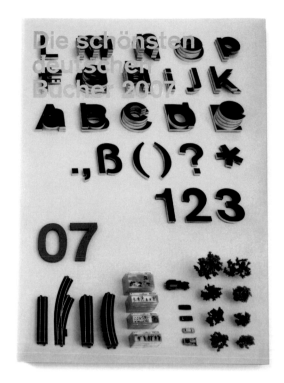

L2M3
Ina Bauer, Frank Geiger, Sascha Lobe,
Thorsten Steidle

Schönste deutsche Bücher 2007

Publication presenting a journey through
the German bookscape. Laid out next to
each other, the characteristic style of layout
becomes visible, while details are shown
in large format. Set pieces from the world
of model railways create enactments that
explore the content of the various books.

Client / Publisher Stiftung Buchkunst Frankfurt
am Main und Leipzig
Editor Uta Scheider
Credits Photography by Ina Bauer, Thorsten Steidle,
supported by Wolfram Palmer

**PIXELGARTEN
& ANDREAS LIEDTKE**

[01] **Beef Magazine**

Client / Publisher Horizont Publishing, ADC Germany

[02] Versuchsanordnungen des Erzählens

Book about Alexander Kluge's process
of Storytelling.

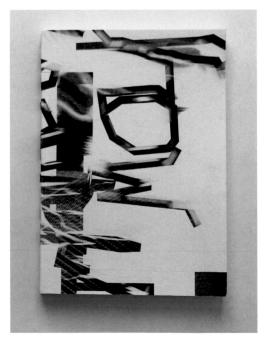

[01]
[02]

New York **RICHARD MEIER**

The architectural authority on all things white gets his fingers dirty.

Meier

Interview by HORACIO SILVA, Photography by KATJA RAHLWES.

RICHARD MEIER

London **DAVID KOHN**

Proud eclecticist builds only houses you can live in.

Interview by CAROLINE ROUX, Photography by DEVIN BLAIR, Styling by SEBASTIAN KAUFMANN.

DAVID KOHN

New York

The perpetual non-conformist has the last laugh.

JAMES WINES

PANORAMA—
Expo '70 Osaka
An avant-garde flashback to Kenzo Tange's architectural Valley of the Dolls.

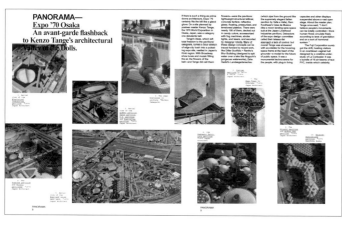

PANORAMA

BEIJING/NEW YORK—
Ole Scheeren
For PIN–UP, the master-mind behind China's state TV headquarters reflects on architecture, life, and fashion. Photography by Julika Rudelius, styling by James Valeri.

OLE SCHEEREN

ETTORE SOTTSASS

[03]
[04]

PIN–UP

Featuring Thierry Mugler 1980, Robert Wilson, Wör-litz, Tina Di Carlo, Julius Shulman, the Hong Kong Cultural Center, Gandalf Gavin and Bald Vogues.

Magazine for Architectural Entertainment
Issue 3, F/W 2007-2008
US$10.00/EUR9.90

ISSN 19339755

9 771933 975000

LOS ANGELES
Julius Shulman—The 97-year old living legend of modern photography shares his passion for architecture—and gardening— with a young Los Angeles architect. Text by Fritz Haeg, Photography by Todd Cole.

1. A large poster with Shulman's name hangs by the entry door to Shulman's main house.

2. A view along the glass wall into the garden outside of Shulman's living room. The house was designed in 1949 by Raphael Soriano.

3. (Right) Perched high on the hills above hectic Los Angeles, Shulman's house is a sleepy refuge of green serenity.

JULIUS SHULMAN
40

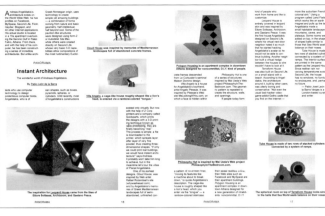

JAMES WINES

Interview by
MICHAEL
BULLOCK,
Photography by
MIGUEL
VILLALOBOS.

JAMES WINES

Magazine for Architectural Entertainment.

Publisher FEBU Publishing LLC
Editor Pierre-Alexandre de Looz

4. A sign above Shulman's crowded desk reads: "Old age and treachery will overcome youth and skill."

5. The stairs to the entrance of the main building is protected by a wall of steel-framed frosted glass.

JULIUS SHULMAN
41

[05|06]
[07|08]

PIN–UP
Featuring PETER MARINO, BEN VAN BERKEL, KEN KELLOGG, R&SIE(N), WILLIAM KATAVOLOS, DAVID ADJAYE, and SAADABAD.
MAGAZINE FOR ARCHITECTURAL ENTERTAINMENT
ISSUE 5 Fall Winter 08/09
US$ 10.00
EUR 9.90
With a special tribute to HERBERT MUSCHAMP.

PIN–UP
Featuring interviews with Jürgen Mayer H., Daniel Arsham, Zaha Hadid, Rick Owens, and Anca Tioreva.

PIN–UP

PIN–UP
Featuring Annabelle Selldorf, Christian Lacroix, Madelon Vriesendorp, Roger Bundschuh, Florian Slotawa, Lustron, Hotel Estela, EXYZT, Brussels, and Aranda/Lasch.

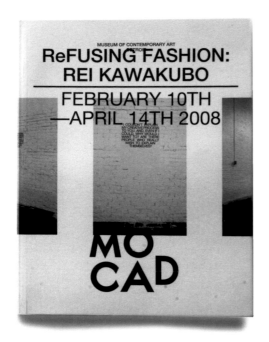

[01]

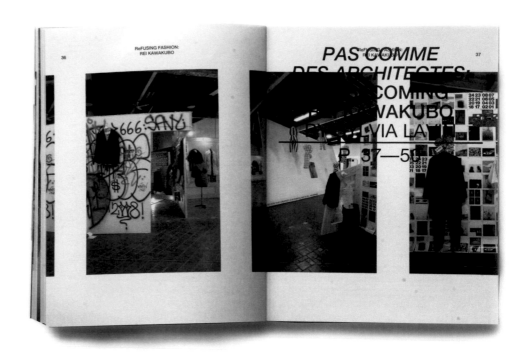

DANIELLE AUBERT & LANA CAVAR

[01] ReFusing Fashion: Rei Kawakubo

Book commemorating the exhibition *ReFusing Fashion: Rei Kawakubo* at the Museum of Contemporary Art Detroit.

GUNMAD
Mads Freund Brunse &
Gudmundur Ulfarsson

[02] Krabbesholm 99–100

Book for for the Danish Folke-Højskole Krabbesholm featuring historical texts, essays, poems and art work.

Client / Publisher Krabbesholm Højskole

DANIELLE AUBERT & LANA CAVAR

[03] ReFusing Fashion: Rei Kawakubo
exhibition guide

Poster made available to visitors to the exhibition. When folded it served as a gallery guide with information about the show and related events.

Client / Publisher Museum of Contemporary Art Detroit
Editors Linda Dresner, Susanne Hilberry, Marsha Miro
Credits Photography by Corine Vermeulen Smith

[02]

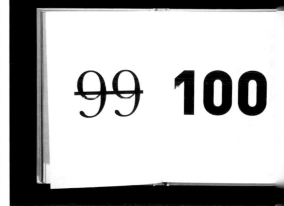

VIER5
P. 178 – 181

Marco Fiedler and Achim Reichert were born and bred in the southern German state of Baden-Wuerttemberg. Together they form design studio *Vier5*. Resolutely opposed to all categorisation, even giving away their age is a classification that goes too far.

Meeting as teenagers at school, they went on to graduate from Design University HFG Offenbach am Main, though they prefer not to divulge their areas of study or years of graduation.

Vier5 have been based in Paris for the last seven years, though their work is not confined to the studio and they spend much of their time in the offices of their country house. More than happy to displace themselves entirely should a project require it, Fiedler and Reichert moved to Kassel for a year in order to complete their work on the guiding system for *Documenta 12*. This way, they explain, "you get deeper and deeper into the theme, you have ideas, you think about materials, about people you can work with and in the end you have one idea and you focus on this idea until it is realised."

Projects include editorial, print, identity and web design for cultural clients including the Museum of Applied Art, Frankfurt; CAC (Centre of Contemporary Art), Bretigny and the Museum of Modern Art, Paris. Still, personal projects are also important to the duo and, since 2003, they have edited and published their own fashion magazine *Fairytale*. Widely available and advertising-free, *Fairytale* is published twice a year.

—
VIER5
Marco Fiedler & Achim Reichert

[01, 03, 05] FAIRY TALE Magazine – issue *Interieur and Architecture*

[02, 04] FAIRY TALE Magazine – issue *Fashion, Beauty and Style*

Editor / Publisher VIER5

[01]

[02]

[03]

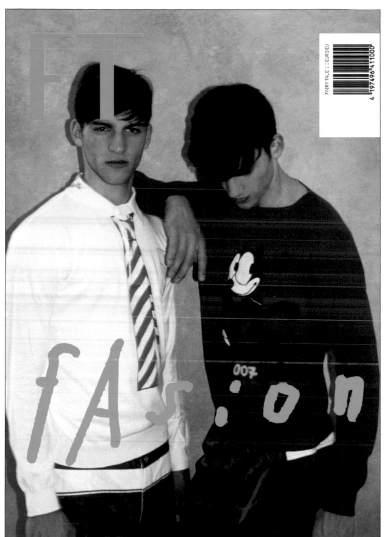

FT

fASion

FT

ARCHIT and
ECTURE interieur

 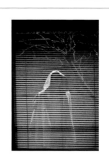   

BED

PAUL MPAGI SEPUYA

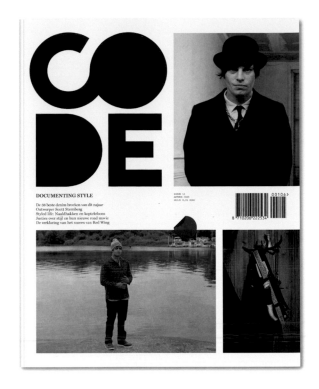

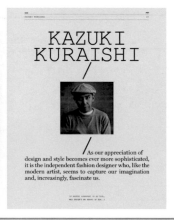

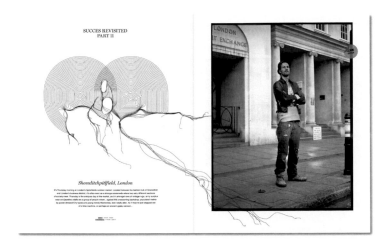

TOKO DESIGN

Code Magazine, Documenting Style

Logo design, layout and art direction for
street fashion magazine.

Client / Publisher Code Magazine BV
Editor Peter van Rhoon

[01]

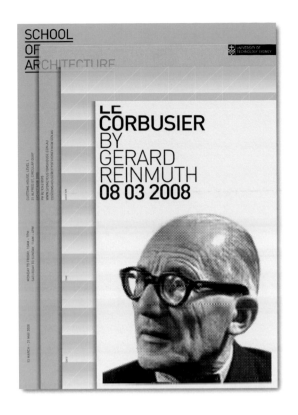

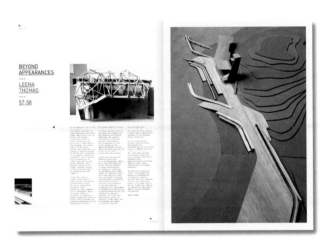

[02]

[03]

—
TOKO DESIGN

Poster, catalogue and flyer for the School of Architecture. The identity is based on 4 colours, each representing one of the four subjects in the Master of Architecture course.

Client UTS School of Architecture

188

—
ONLAB
Nicolas Bourquin

Gazette – Tramelan change de couleurs

Three issues of a newspaper communicat-
ing the new visual identity of the city of
Tramelan exclusively to its inhabitants. The
first issue is related to the "way of life", the
second is based on "knowledge" and the
third presents the "know-how". The content
grows with each issue.

Client / Editor / Publisher City of Tramelan, Switzerland
Material / Print Technique Inkjet b/w photos, 5 colour print
Credits Concept, Art Direction, Graphic Design, Text
and Interviews by Nicolas Bourquin, Thibaud Tissot / Photography by onlab and Joël Tettamanti

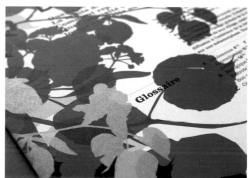

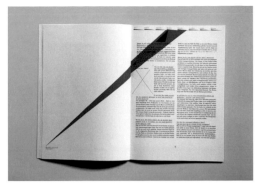

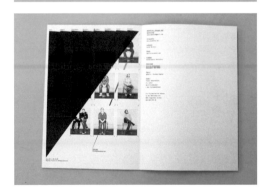
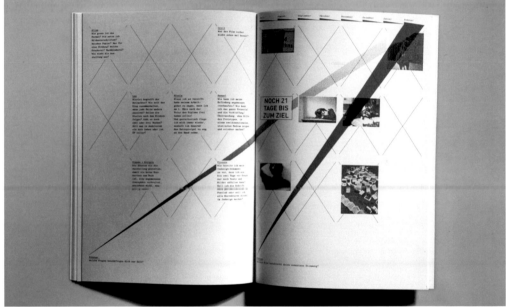
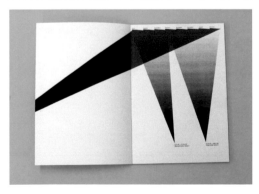

—
PIROL
Ruth Amstutz

Es ist eine ziemlich konstruierte Situation

Diploma book for the study course Visual
Communication at the Academy of
Arts, Bern.

Client Diplomklasse 2008 Visuelle Kommunikation,
Hochschule der Künste Bern
Editor / Publisher Ruth Amstutz
Credits Portraits by Gina Folly / Print by Rollo Press

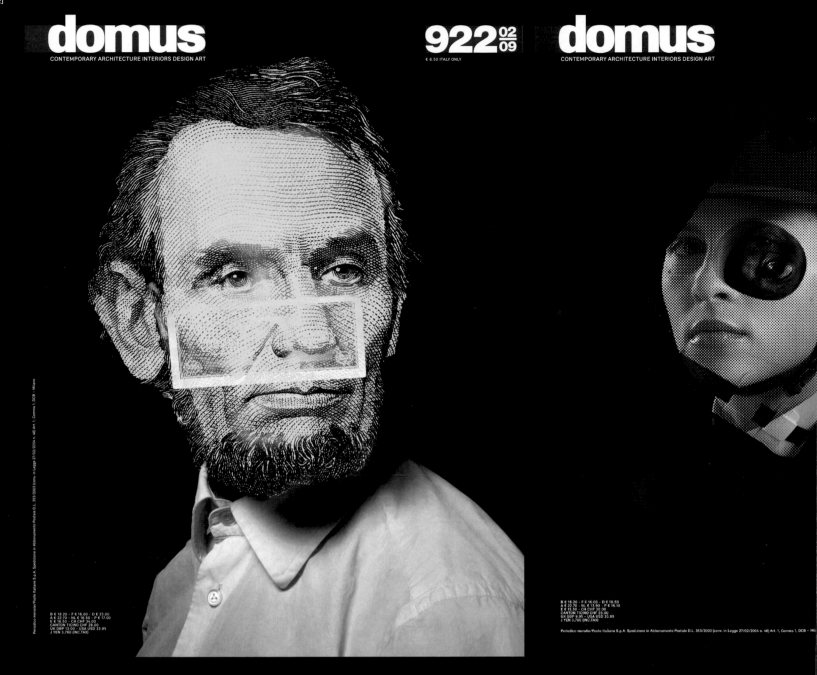

B € 18.20 - F € 16.00 - D € 23.00
A € 22.70 - NL € 16.50 - P € 17.00
E € 16.50 - CH CHF 34.00
CANTON TICINO CHF 28.00
UK GBP 13.00 - USA USD 33.95
J YEN 3,780 (INC.TAX)

922 02/09

€ 8.50 ITALY ONLY

B € 18.20 - F € 16.00 - D € 18.50
A € 22.70 - NL € 13.90 - P € 16.10
E € 15.50 - CH CHF 30.00
CANTON TICINO CHF 28.00
UK GBP 9.95 - USA USD 33.95
J YEN 3,780 (INC.TAX)

Periodico mensile/Poste Italiane S.p.A. Spedizione in Abbonamento Postale D.L. 353/2003 (conv. in Legge 27/02/2004 n. 46) Art. 1, Comma 1, DCB – Mil

913 04/08

€ 8.50 ITALY ONLY

ONLAB
Nicolas Bourquin

Domus Redesign, Cover Principle

Cover re-design for magazine constructed
with its "outer" cover, the wrapping. The
overlapping of the two images produces a
third. The image on the plastic film vanishes
with the act of unwrapping the magazine,
with the removal and disposal of its outer
cover.

Client / Publisher Editoriale Domus, Italy
Credits Creative Direction and Concept by onlab,
Nicolas Bourquin, Sven Ehmann / Graphic Design
by onlab, Nicolas Bourquin, Linda Hintz, Thibaud
Tissot / Graphic Design Assistance by onlab,
Marie-Louise Greb, Yvonne Schneider / Type
Design by Mika Mischler

[07]

domus
CONTEMPORARY ARCHITECTURE INTERIORS DESIGN ART

914 05/08

€ 8.50 ITALY ONLY

[08]

Periodico mensile/Poste Italiane S.p.A. Spedizione in Abbonamento Postale D.L. 353/2003 (conv. in Legge 27/02/2004 n. 46) Art. 1, Comma 1, DCB – Milano

B € 18.20 - F € 16.00 - D € 18.50
A € 22.70 - NL € 13.90 - P € 16.10
E € 15.50 - CH CHF 30.00
CANTON TICINO CHF 28.00
UK GBP 13.00 - USA USD 33.95
J YEN 3,780 (INC.TAX)

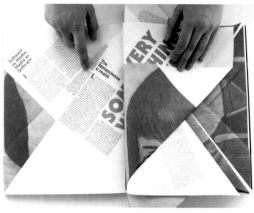
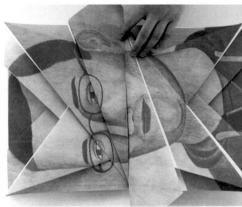

—
ONLAB
Nicolas Bourquin

Domus Intersections, Issue 923 March 2009

Section of 24 pages within the issue of a magazine, binded between stories of the magazine. A folding-principle was developed specifically for the printed form of the magazine. The layout follows the folding marks, whereas the two languages are placed at directly opposed angles.

Client / Publisher Editoriale Domus, Italy
Editors Stefania Garassini, Loredana Mascheroni
Credits Creative Direction and Concept by onlab, Nicolas Bourquin, Sven Ehmann / Graphic Design by onlab, Nicolas Bourquin, Thibaud Tissot, Maike Hamacher, Barbara Hofmann / Illustrations by Tobias Krafczyk

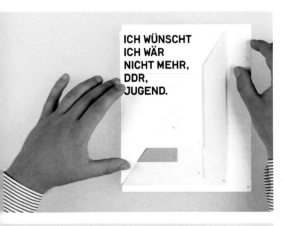

KONRAD RENNER

Ich wünscht ich wär nicht mehr, DDR, JUGEND

Book dealing with the phenomenon of disappearance.

Credits Burg Giebichenstein, University of Art and Design, Halle, Department of Visual Communication / Instruction by Prof. Anna Berkenbusch, Dipl. Des. Manja Hellpap

—
NIESSEN & DE VRIES

Toeval Gezocht

This book is the result of an art education
project involving 325 children, 15 artists and
15 schools. In this project a study was made
into the connection between the expressive
language of children and the artistic languages of sculptors Heringa/Van Kalsbeek,
who make sculptures where controlled ac-
cidents play a large role.

Client Stichting Toeval gezocht
Publisher Lemnscaat

THE SUM IS ALWAYS GREATER THAN THE PARTS.

CALLE ENSTRÖM

The sum is always greater than the parts.

Series of posters for Forsbergs School of Design.

Client Forsbergs School of Design

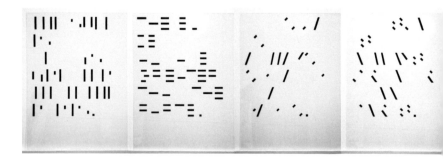

—
HELMO
Thomas Couderc & Clément Vauchez
[01–02] Fresco for "Rock'n'Roll 1954–1959" exhibition
in Fondation Cartier, art Center in Paris

Graphic 150 metres fresco for an
exhibition.

Client Fondation Cartier pour l'art contemporain
Credits Technical Collaboration by Alice Guillier,
Thomas Dimetto, Ivan Legal

—
SANDA ZAHIROVIC
& LAURA MINGOZZI

[03] Royal Opera House

Three advertising prints encouraging
the public to visit the Royal Opera House
website.

—
MARGARET WARZECHA
& GODA BUDVYTYTE

[04] Gerrit Rietveld Academie Graduation Show of
the Graphic Design Department

Poster design for the graduation show using
A2 posters as the only element. The basic
layer consisted of five designs which were
each offset-printed in four different colours.

Client Graphic Design Department, Gerrit Rietveld
Academie, Amsterdam
Credits Kasper Andreasen

—
KAI-TING LIN

[05] IS IT NOW IS IT YOU

Poster and invite for the design symposium *Is
It Now? Is It You?*

Client Designlab

[01]

[02]

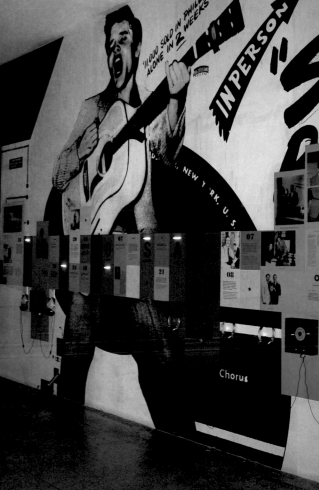

[03]

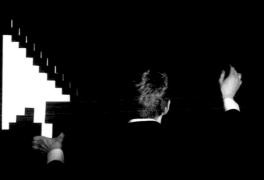

WWW.ROYALOPERA.ORG

WWW.ROYALOPERA.ORG

weiner
l3

Josel

Vito
Acconci
34

Green
with envy

Feeling
blue

Silken
lies

A velvet
voice

Grimmer
Grimm
Grim
Grimmer
Grimm
Grim

Vito
Acconc
34

BIANCA
MANZANA
DE AGUSTIN
& SEMUEL
SOUHUWAT

FASHION
SHOW

[01]

CONTAINER PLUS

[01] The Assembly website

Website for a boutique advertising agency. Each character of the website has an individual hand-made quality and moves and appears on the screen in a different manner.

Client The Assembly
Credits Web design by Rufus Kahler

SERIAL CUT
Sergio del Puerto

[02] +H2o-Co2

[03] Ecology

Poster graphics for the CO₂ reduction campaign of a company that designs sinks, water tanks and water-saving devices. 3D-based compositions use type blocks and combine them with natural elements.

Client Roca

SERIAL CUT
Sergio del Puerto

[04] Mediterranean Summer Mood

Still life billboards for the promotion campaign of a Spanish beer brand. Their original logo and star are real live objects in the scene.

Client Estrella Damm
Credits Photography by Paloma Rincón for Villar Rosas

[05] PopUp Trains – Media Distancia

Billboards for the campaign of a Spanish train company using pop-up books with different backgrounds.

Client Renfe (Spain)
Credits Photography by Paloma Rincón or TBWA Madrid

NIESSEN & DE VRIES

[01] Nests / Nester

Self-commissioned book that has turned into an assembly kit for a mini-exhibition reporting the artist's working method.

Editor Niessen & de Vries
Publisher Uitgeverij Boek

MATTIS DOVIER

[02] Extrusion

3-dimensional posters made by using the numerical filter called "extrusion" on Photoshop, which plays on the decomposition of the picture with a degree of abstraction according to the perspective of the point of view.

[04] 3D / Print Poster

3-dimensional poster playing on two different typefaces, the volume of one and the print of the other.

SANDA ZAHIROVIC

[03] Totally Space Opera

Ten book covers for a set of science fiction books.

Publisher Gollancz / Orion Publishing Group
Credits Creative Direction by Lucie Stericker

[01]

[02]

CENTURY RAIN
ALISTAIR REYNOLDS

GREG BEAR

TAU ZERO
POUL ANDERSON

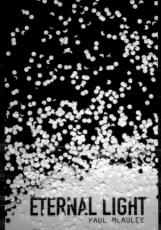

ETERNAL LIGHT
PAUL McAULEY

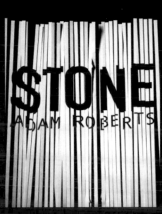

STONE
ADAM ROBERTS

RENDEZVOUS
WITH RAMA
ARTHUR C. CLARKE

ILIUM
DAN SIMMONS

RINGWORLD
LARRY NIVEN

LAST AND
FIRST MEN
OLAF STAPLEDON

CENTAURI
DEVICE
M. JOHN HARRISON

POSTER

DAMIEN POULAIN

Damien Poulain was born in Angers, France in 1975. He was educated at four different schools. First he studied Visual Communication at the Institut d'Arts Visuels in Orleans, then at the Ecole Nationale Supérieure des Beaux Arts in Nancy. Thirdly in Toulouse, where he attended the Ecole Supérieure des Beaux Arts, and finally at the Staatliche Akademie der Bildenden Künste in Stuttgart, Germany, from where he graduated in 2000.

It was as a teenager that Poulain first realised he wanted to become a commercial artist. "I was fascinated by graphic designers," he explains. "I could see design was influencing theatre, cinema, fashion, and everything else around us. This intrigued me and I became curious."

Having lived and worked in Spain, Germany and Italy (at *Fabrica*, the Benetton Group Communications Research Center), Poulain finally chose London in 2002 for, he jokes, "the fog, the expensive rents and the warm sun."

While clients include *Dazed & Confused* magazine and Adidas, Poulain particularly enjoys projects for which he is author, namely: *Rodeo* magazine, Nike, for whom he created shop windows and Uniqlo, for their promotional magazines.

"When working on a project, initially I try to exchange ideas with my clients as much as possible" he says of the design process. "After this it's all about problem solving, both conceptually and visually." "I love the hand-made and the machine-fabricated so I use different tools," he continues. "I like human imperfection so it's all about balancing this with new technology."

DAMIEN POULAIN

[01–02] Uniqlo paper 4

Three illustrations to introduce the cities of Tokyo, New York and London for a magazine.

Client / Publisher Uniqlo
Credits Photography by Lacey

[03] 55DSL

Installation celebrating Renzo Rosso's birthday year.

Client / Publisher Arena Homme +

[04] The Guardian / Science Fiction and Fantasy supplement

[05] The Guardian / Crime supplement

[06] The Guardian / War and Travel supplement

Illustration for a series of seven covers for the supplement of a newspaper.

Client / Publisher The Guardian
Credits Photography by Lacey

theguardian **TheObserver** | 23.01.2009

1000 NOVELS EVERYONE MUST READ

**Volume 7
War & Travel**

JULIAN BITTINER

Born in 1973 to British parents in Geneva, Anglo-Swiss designer Julian Bittiner is currently based in New Haven, Connecticut. His work, he says, "is focused primarily in the cultural sector and is characterised by an interest in the greater context of art and design, and its relationship to our social environment."

Ironically, considering his Swiss upbringing, it was not until he was at the Art Center College of Design in Pasadena, California, from where he graduated first with a bachelor's degree in Fine Art in 1995, that Bittiner became aware of graphic design as a discipline.

"Sometimes I wonder if this might be attributed to my growing up in the Swiss-French rather than the Swiss-German area where almost all the pivotal figures of that time practiced," Bittiner explains. "However," he is quick to add, "I think my general aesthetic proclivities and ethos have been heavily influenced by Swiss culture at large."

And so, it was not until the mid-1990s, and in the United States, that a copy of influential magazine, *Emigre* (issue 37), would pique Bittiner's design curiosity.

"The synthesis of critical reflection, visual experimentation and independent publishing," he tells us, "pointed to a social and accessible form of art that is still the basis of my attraction to the discipline."

Bittiner went on to graduate with a bachelor's degree in Graphic Design from the very same school four years later. Then, after several years of working professionally as a designer, went back to school again, to graduate just this past year with a Master's degree in Graphic Design from the Yale School of Art, where he now also lectures part-time.

Bittiner is inspired by individuals: people he describes as "independent and original thinkers/makers with a strong sense of who they are, what they want, and why they do what they do," from Bertrand Russell to the Beatles.

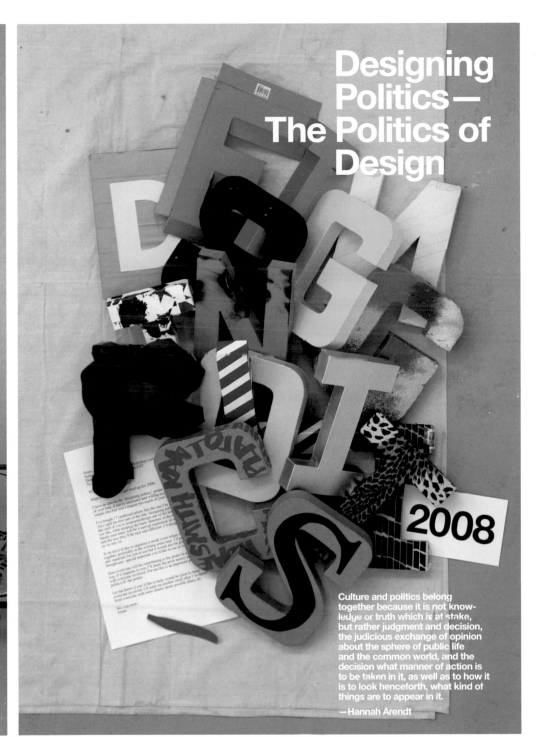

Designing Politics—
The Politics of
Design

2008

Culture and politics belong
together because it is not knowledge or truth which is at stake,
but rather judgment and decision,
the judicious exchange of opinion
about the sphere of public life
and the common world, and the
decision what manner of action is
to be taken in it, as well as to how it
is to look henceforth, what kind of
things are to appear in it.
—Hannah Arendt

JULIAN BITTINER & RYAN WALLER

[01] Jürg Lehni Workshop

Poster announcing a workshop by Jürg
Lehni and Uli Franke in conjunction with
an exhibition at the Yale School of Art.

Client / Publisher Yale School of Art
Credits Photography by Colin Smith

[04] Hektor Games

Poster series created for Jürg Lehni and
Uli Franke's workshop at the Yale School
of Art.

Client Yale School of Art

JULIAN BITTINER

[02–03] Designing Politics – The Politics of Design

Poster for an international poster
competition.

Client 2008 Ulm International Forum
poster competition

[05] Pierre Huyghe: Unbirthday Present

Poster announcing a lecture by Pierre
Huyghe at the Yale School of Art.

Client Yale School of Art

JULIAN BITTINER,
RYAN WALLER, JÜRG LEHNI &
ULI FRANKE

[06] Hektor Workshop

Poster for a workshop by Jürg Lehni and
Uli Franke in conjunction with an exhibition at the Yale School of Art.

Client / Publisher Yale School of Art

[05|06]

À 2 C'EST MIEUX

Rendez-vous sauvage,
un cabinet de curiosités mobile

Truck turned into an ambulant contemporary art gallery including poster-invitation card, press release book, stickers, website for an art event.

Client Rendez-vous sauvage

À 2 C'EST MIEUX

Wild Posters in Chaumont

Large format fresco posters for a festival in Chaumont.

Client Association Des Oh et des Bah!

[01|02|03]

À 2 C'EST MIEUX

[01]   Rendez-vous sauvage / 1,2,3 GO!

[02]   Rendez-vous sauvage / ON AIR

[03]   Rendez-vous sauvage / Niveaux de Gris Poster Collection

Poster for an ambulant contemporary art gallery.

Client Rendez-vous sauvage

TU SAIS QUI ™

[01] **Cabaret Martyr**

Poster for Cabaret Martyr, a Parisian
electro-cabaret show.

Client La Loge

[02] **Svetlana & Viktor's wedding stage**

Stage design and scenography for
a wedding ceremony.

Client Svetlana & Viktor Antonov

[next spread]

TU SAIS QUI ™

The You Know Who

Credits Photography by Raphaël Dautigny

[01]

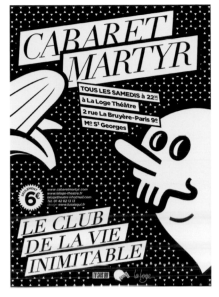

[02]

[01|02]

[03]

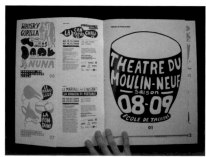

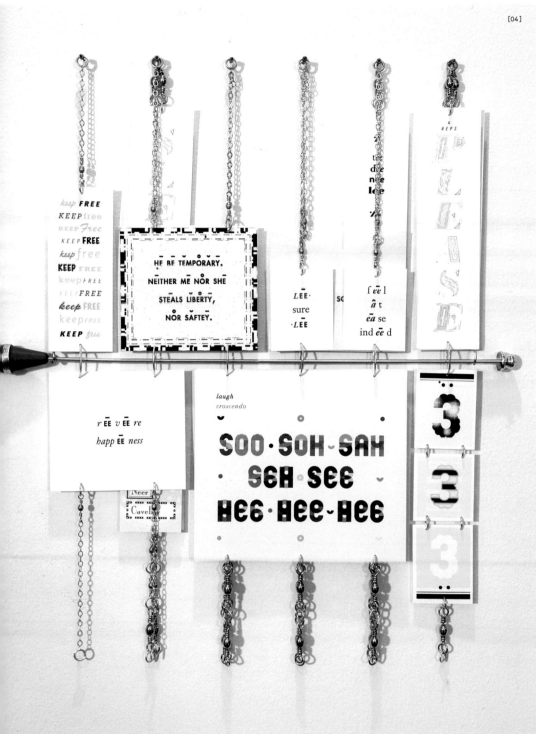

[04]

FROMKEETRA
Keetra Dean Dixon

[04] Euphora-Phonics Drill Set:
Exercises in "ee" & "ah"

Exercises to simulate the 42 smiling muscles.
A system of cards as part of a serial install-
ment. The Euphora-Phonics Drill Set was
inspired by scientific studies showing that
positive emotion and cooler facial tempera-
tures result when people say the letter E or
the sound AH over and over again due to the
fact that forming these sounds requires a
smile-like expression.

[05] Cordial Invitations

Type of Work Series of postcards

[05]

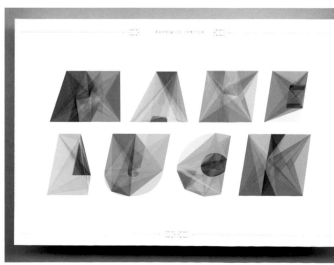

HAPPYPETS PRODUCTS

[01] Happypets swiss-bunker (inside)
installation

Installation for an exhibition at the
Breda Graphic design museum curated by
Erik Kessels.

[02] Photography of our studio

Credits Photography by Marko Stevic / ECAL

[03] Season programme 2008–2009

Flyers, posters, catalogue and T-shirt
designed for a season programme.

ILLUSTRA-TION

Illustration has established itself again as a design discipline in its own right. Conventional illustrative advertising graphics had been displaced by advertising photography using four-colour printing technology in the 1960s and 1970s, but this design discipline made a comeback in the 1990s with fashion illustration and character design, and has maintained its position ever since. Graphic designers value the qualities of illustration as a design tool which gives their works a personal, human touch. Hard-drawn sketches and illustrations help to counteract and modify the "perfect" designs generated by computers, which often create a slightly cold impression. This holds particularly in the area of typography. Graphic designers are continuing to develop display fonts and create illustrative fonts. Hand-made, customised illustrative letterforms lend graphic designs an emotional identity.

[01]

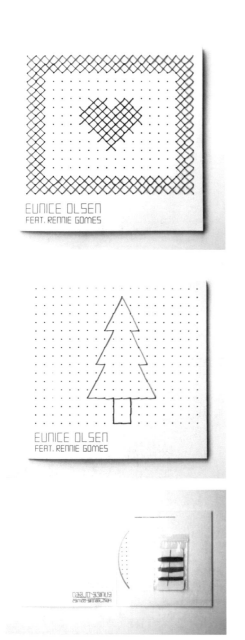

[02]

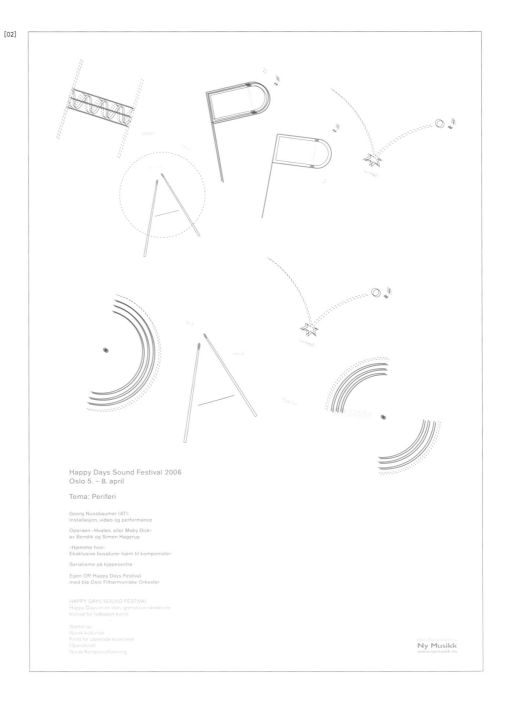

Happy Days Sound Festival 2006
Oslo 5. – 8. april

Tema: Periferi

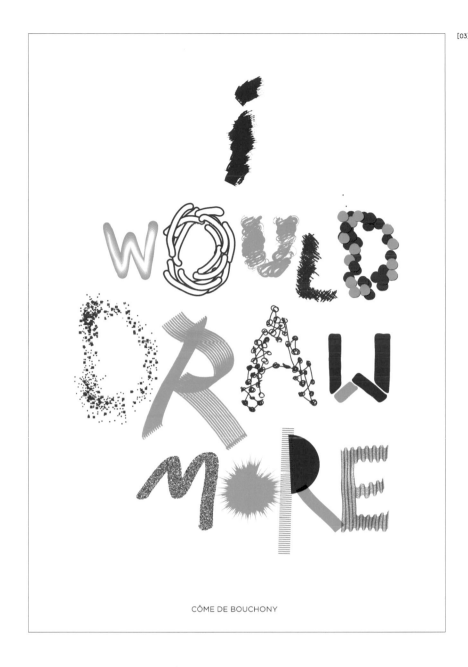

CÔME DE BOUCHONY

CÔME DE BOUCHONY

Côme de Bouchony was born in Paris in 1984. He graduated with a degree in Graphic Design just 2 years ago in 2007 from ESAG (École Supérieure d'Arts Graphiques) Penninghen, also in Paris. The course included a year's study in Rotterdam at the Willem de Kooning Academy.

Having set up his own studio soon after graduating, De Bouchony now works from home, though he is currently looking for shared studio space. Though his original ambition was to become a product designer, De Bouchony explains that while at Penninghen, "I discovered form, colour, composition, typography and art direction" and so, sufficiently seduced, decided to switch to graphic design.

Working mainly with digital tools in both print and motion design, and with a particular interest in typography, clients so far have included *The New York Times*, Franco-German TV channel *Arte*, *Wad* magazine and record labels *Uppercuts* and *Mental Groove*. De Bouchony's dream job, however, would be "to create and art direct a forward thinking art, music, style and politics magazine". He cites music as his main inspiration.

"When it comes to my commissioned work," De Bouchony explains of his design process, "I usually have a pretty clear idea of the feeling and the atmosphere I want to communicate." "I start by thinking a lot about the possibilities and what I want to achieve, until I reach a certain point when I feel ready to simplify things," he continues. "At this point, I can actually make the project without thinking too much. Most often, though, the final piece is nothing like my original idea. I guess I like to surprise myself."

Côme de bouchony 2008

[01]

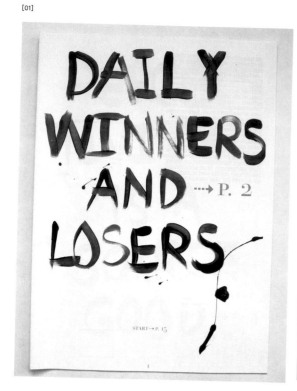

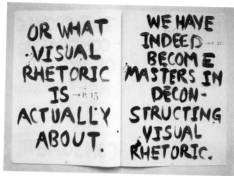

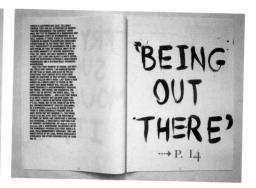

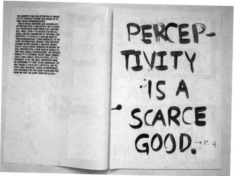

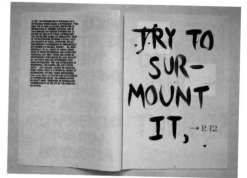

[02]
[03|04]

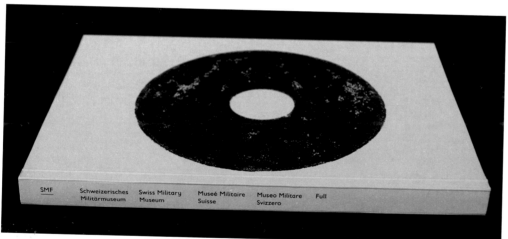

[01]
L
P
P
Cli

H
[02]
L
T
f
C

[03]
I

KAREN VAN DE KRAATS

[01] Producing Attention

Book commissioned by Onomatopee
for a series of publications on visual rhetoric.

Client / Publisher Onomatopee Publishers
Editor Rudi Laermans

HANNES GLOOR & STEFAN JANDL

[02] Sierra Mike Foxtrott

Publication that is a mixture between catalogue, inventory, satire and art book.

Editor Stefan Jandl & Jonas Niedermann

[03] Astoria – Praktiken des Sekundären

Book as a visual research divided into three
parts – archival-, reproductive- and imi-
tative practices.

Editor Hannes Gloor

SIMONA BRÜHLMEIER
& FREDERIK LINKE

[04] Des Wahnsinns fette Beute –
The fat booty of madness

Book containing the first complete survey
of training and education in jewelry making
at Munich Art Academy from 1991 to the
present, with over 1000 illustrations and
biographies of all contributing students.

Client Pinakothek der Moderne, München
Editor Dr. Florian Hufnagl
Publisher Arnoldsche Art Publishers

DAVID ISAKSSON, ANDERS LÖVGREN,
MARTIN NICOLAUSSON &
JONAS NORDIN

[05] Beckmans College of Design Graduation Show

Client Beckmans College of Design

SACHA LEOPOLD

[06] B.A.T.

Posters for the B.A.T project.: Bon A Tirer (Ready to be printed) a response to a report stating that it was impossible for the talented printing officers to create or express themselves. The idea is to give voice to those who are usually only repeating the same action and also to try to restore a value to posters produced in large series by introducing uniqueness and difference.

STUDIOSPASS
Jaron Korvinus & Daan Mens

[07] Drukwerk buiten de marge

Promotional printwork for *Drukwerk Buiten de marge*, an exhibition on graphic art in the 3rd and 4th dimension.

Client Pictura, Dordrecht 2009

[05]

[06]

[07]

[01]   Illustration

Advertising company's identity illustration.

Client Ads-Click
Editor / Publisher Bread and Butter SA

[02]   Bella Vita Factoria

Client / Editor / Publisher Le Couloir

—
THEMES
Mathias Forbach & Thomas Koenig

[03]   Lucky Joy

Client / Editor / Publisher Lucky Joy

—
THEMES
Thomas Koenig, Eva Lauterlein,
Mathias Forbach

[04]   The Mondrians

CD sleeve design made of a 3D photography
of an installation.

Client / Editor / Publisher The Mondrians
Credits Photography by Eva Lauterlein

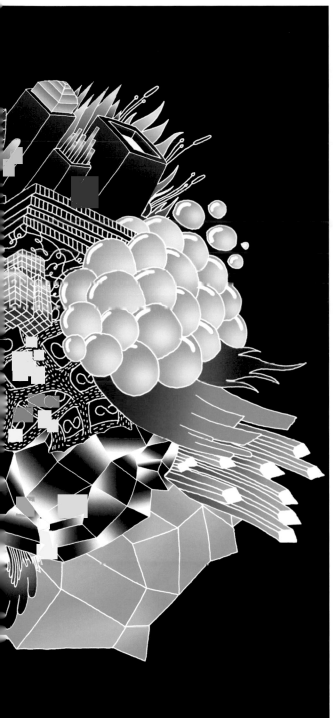

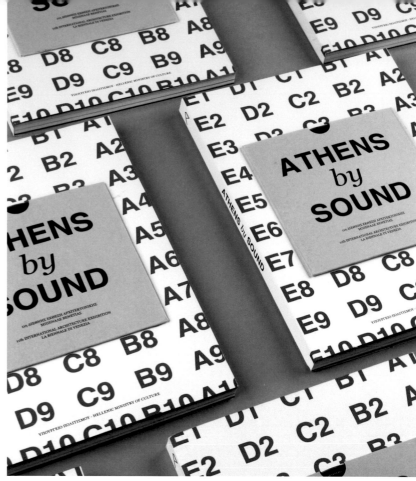

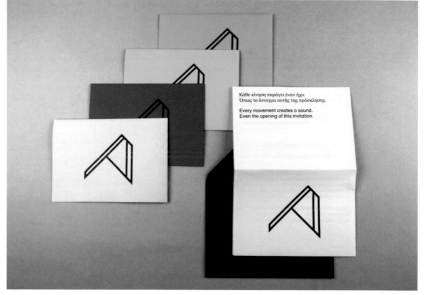

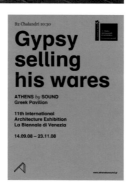

238

[01]

—
COMPANY

[01]   ATHENS by SOUND

Book with invitations, posters, flyers and
catalogue for the Greek Pavilion at the 11th
Architecture Biennale in Venice. The winning
Greek project, "Athens by Sound" created
an interactive map of the city's soundscape.
Playing on the idea that visitors should listen
rather than look, the posters used simple
typography to describe five typical Athenian
sounds –church bells, screeching brakes –
written in oversized letters that shout out to
passers by in the street.

Client Hellenic Ministry of Culture
Editor Christina Achtypi Stelios Giamarelos Anasta-
sia Karandinou
Publisher Futura
Credits Art Direction by Company

—
COUP
Erica Terpstra & Peter van den Hoogen

[02]   Pioneers

Banner for a Festival presenting young
thinkers and musical acts from Amsterdam
and New York. Featured is a mix of typefaces
found on oldskool New York HipHop flyers
that communicate this festival on the occa-
sion of a 400-year collaboration.

Client Felix Meritis

[03]   Pioneers Flyers

Client Felix Meritis
Editor Linda Kleinhout / Joanneke Lootsma

—
DAMIEN POULAIN &
ANTHONY BURRILL

[04]   2AM

Identity and stationery for London-based
production company 2AM. Made in collaboration with Anthony Burrill.

Client 2AM

[05]   KK Outlet

Identity and stationery for an advertising
agency in London. Made in collaboration
with Anthony Burrill.

Client KK Outlet (KesselsKramer)

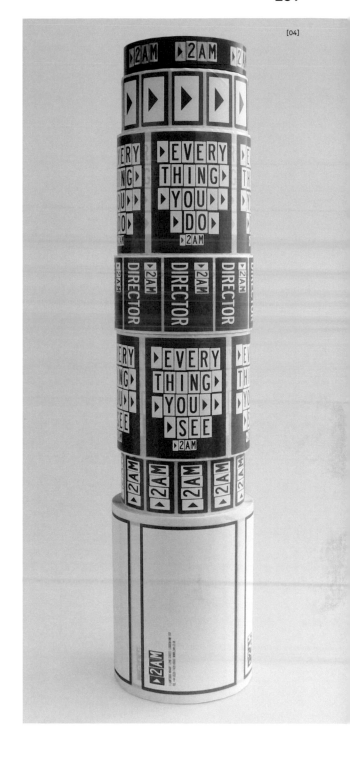

03

LESLIE DAVID

Antisocials Covers

Identity and program for new parties at
the Social Club. The idea was to represent
in one picture all the bands playing there
each month.

Client / Publisher Social Cub

ULTRA:STUDIO
Ludovic Gerber

[01]   Milton Deforge Impression

Poster.

Client Milton Deforge Impression

—

DIEGO FELLAY / ECAL

[02]   Designing under Influence

Book, poster and envrionnement.

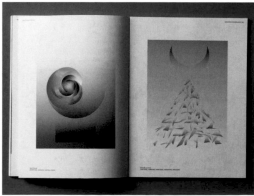

PHIL YAMADA

[01] Rick Valicenti Lecture #1

First version of the Rick Valicenti poster.

[02] Rick Valicenti Lecture #2

The first poster (*Rick Valicenti Lecture #1*)
led to this new version.

JONAS VOEGELI

[03] In der Voliere

Client Peter Radelfinger

BILLY BEN & ANNA HAAS

[04] Concert Posters for Fri-Son Club

Melvins

In Flames

Client Fri-Son

BILLY BEN

[04] Concert Posters for Fri-Son Club

Leila

Adam Green

Joan as Police Woman

Client Fri-Son

HI
Megi Zumstein & Claudio Barandun

[05] Bernhard Willhelm – Het Totaal Rappel

Book of the exhibition of the fashion designer
Bernhard Willhelm at MoMu Antwerp.

Client / Editor / Publisher Modemuseum Antwerpen
Credits Illustration by Claudio Barandun

[01|02]

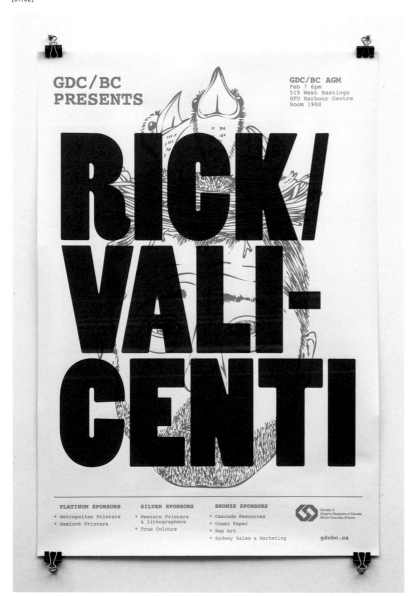

[03]

VOLIERE ZÜRICH
MYTHENQUAI 1
8002 ZÜRICH

SONNTAG
1:
9. November 08
10 – 12 Uhr und
14 – 16 Uhr

SAMSTAG
2:
15. November 08
10 – 12 Uhr und
14 – 16 Uhr

SONNTAG
3:
16. November 08
10 – 12 Uhr und
14 – 16 Uhr

PETER RADELFINGER ZEIGT SEINEN ZEICHENZYKLUS
«ENDLICH KOMM ICH IN DEN ZWITSCHERRAUM»
SCHÖN&GUT IST SCHON DRIN.
CHRISTOPH LANG INSTALLIERT.

IN
DER
VOLIÈRE

[04]

[05]

we hortly invite you to the

4 pm at marion & eikes place
neue kulmer strasse 2
10827 berlin

[02]

FROM PULVER RECORDS / BUDAPEST, HUNGARY

ERIK SUMO AND BAND

SURREALISTIC WORLD MUSIC DANCEFLOOR SOUNDTRACKS   SUPPORTED BY DJ RINGMASTER
FRIDAY SEPTEMBER 29 TH 2006 DOORS 22H
DACHSTOCK REITSCHULE BERN   PRESALE AT ROCKAWAY BEACH, SPEICHERGASSE 25, BERN

[03]

Lucerne University of
Applied Sciences and Arts
HOCHSCHULE
LUZERN

Design & Kunst

FH Zentralschweiz

ANNA HAAS
With and for hort

[01]   X-mas Invitation

Invitation flyer for a private X-mas
dinner. Made out of plain paper and
coloured cordes.

Client / Editor / Publisher Hort
Credits Photography by Ramon Haindl

—

LORENZO GEIGER

[02]   Erik Sumo Poster

Client Dachstock Reitschule Bern

SABINA ALBANESE

[03]   OPEN DAY Poster

Poster inspired by *Cat's Cradle*.

Client Lucerne University of Applied
Sciences and Arts
Credits Photographer: Aki Müller

—

STUDIO SPORT
Ronnie Fueglister & Martin Stoecklin

[04]   The Glue: Kin' de Lele

CD-Cover artwork and promotional material
for the Swiss a-cappella band *The Glue*. The
typeface is made out of scans from the faces
and hands of the band members.

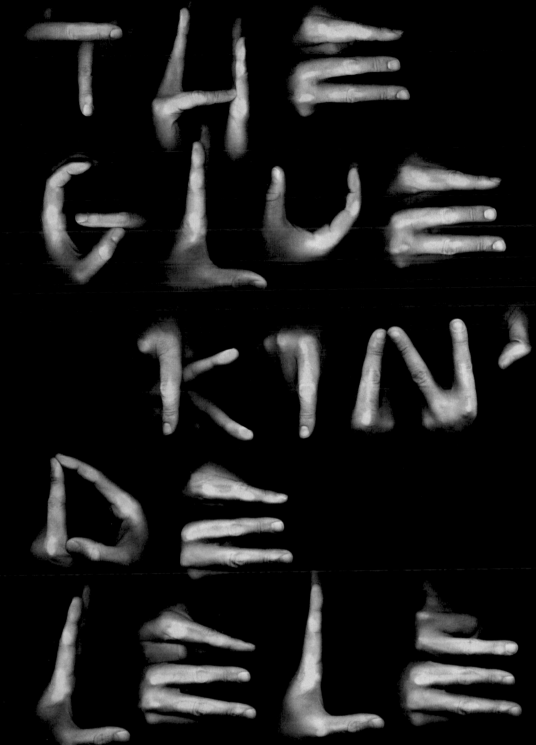

www.theglue.ch

[01|02|03]

 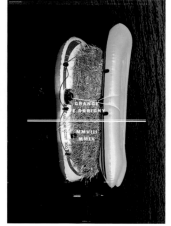 

[04]

—
FEDERAL STUDIO

[01] Le filet
[02] Le bateau
[03] La chaise
[04] La grange
[05] Le lozziworm

Poster for a theater in Switzerland.
Client Theater of La Grange de Dorigny
Credits Art direction & Photography by Régis Golay

PHOTO-GRAPHY

It is interesting to observe the manner in which graphic designers employ photography using a rather conventional conceptual understanding. While designers in the English-speaking world tend to work with image-based concepts, the continental European school traditionally concentrates on typography and conceptual, serial approaches. All of the major identifiable styles in photography over the last 20 years can currently be found in graphic design too: from the fantastic realism of the 1970s, the hyper-real approach of Jürgen Teller, Jeff Wall or early Wolfgang Tillmans, the neo-romantic and neo-surrealistic motifs of the current decade after the style of Erwin Olaf. Graphic designers often work with black-and-white photography, with subtle contrasts dominating. A hazy, granular "photocopied" aesthetic adds to the impression of spontaneity, improvisation, rebellion and subversion. Graphic designers do this in order to give their works an authentic feel.

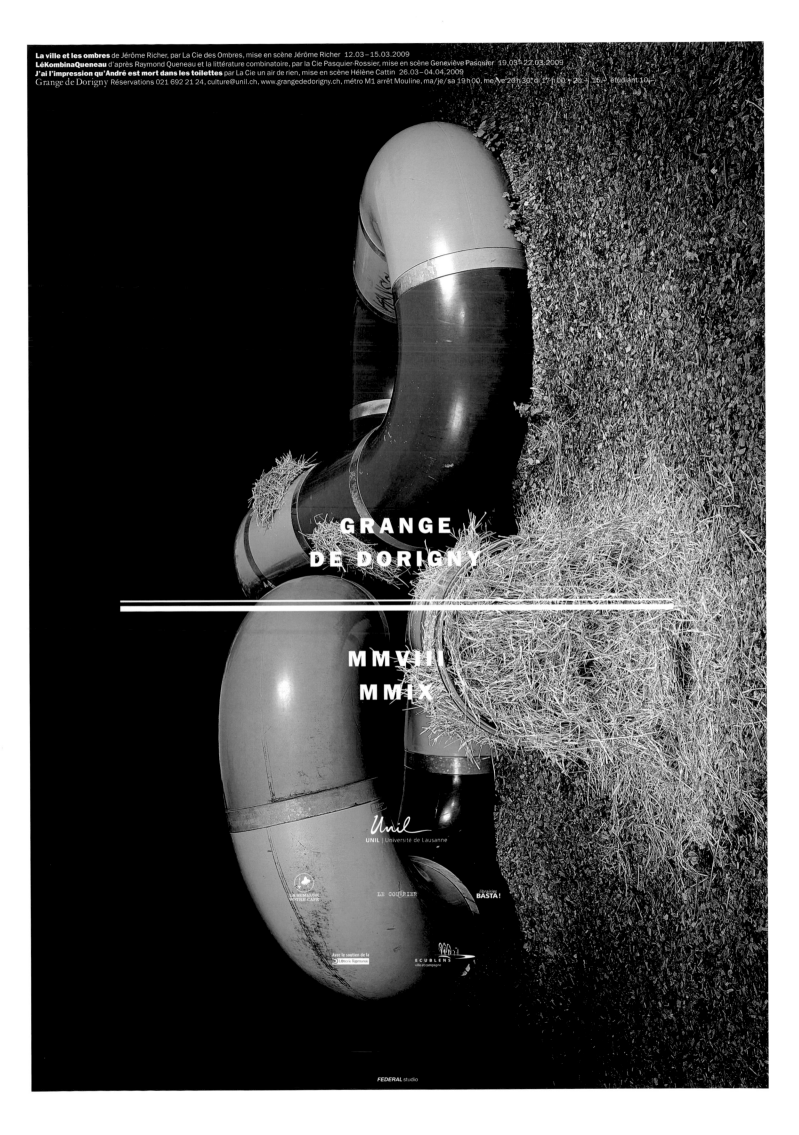

La ville et les ombres de Jérôme Richer, par La Cie des Ombres, mise en scène Jérôme Richer 12.03–15.03.2009
LéKombinaQueneau d'après Raymond Queneau et la littérature combinatoire, par la Cie Pasquier-Rossier, mise en scène Geneviève Pasquier 19.03–22.03.2009
J'ai l'impression qu'André est mort dans les toilettes par La Cie un air de rien, mise en scène Hélène Cattin 26.03–04.04.2009
Grange de Dorigny Réservations 021 692 21 24, culture@unil.ch, www.grangededorigny.ch, métro M1 arrêt Mouline, ma/je/sa 19 h 00, me/ve 20 h 30, di 17 h 00 , 20.– ; 15.– ; étudiant 10.–

GRANGE
DE DORIGNY

MMVIII
MMIX

UNIL | Université de Lausanne

—
SUPERBÜRO
Barbara Ehrbar

[01]   Bieler Fototage 2008

Two promotional camera costumes.

Client Bieler Fototage
Credits Photography by Daniel Mueller

—
STUDIO SPORT
Ronnie Fueglister & Martin Stoecklin

[02]   Lala Blabla Pomme d'Adam

Posters and leaflet for an a-cappella music
festival. A quasi-phonetic image-alphabet
has been developed, showing the shape of
a human mouth while spelling the letters of
the alphabet.

Client / Publisher The Glue Productions GmbH
Editor Studio Sport
Credits Lips by Gina Folly

[01]

5.–28.9.2008

[ ]

JOURNÉES PHOTOGRAPHIQUES DE BIENNE
BIELER FOTOTAGE

WWW.JOUPH.CH
WWW.BIELERFOTOTAGE.CH

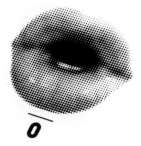

[02]

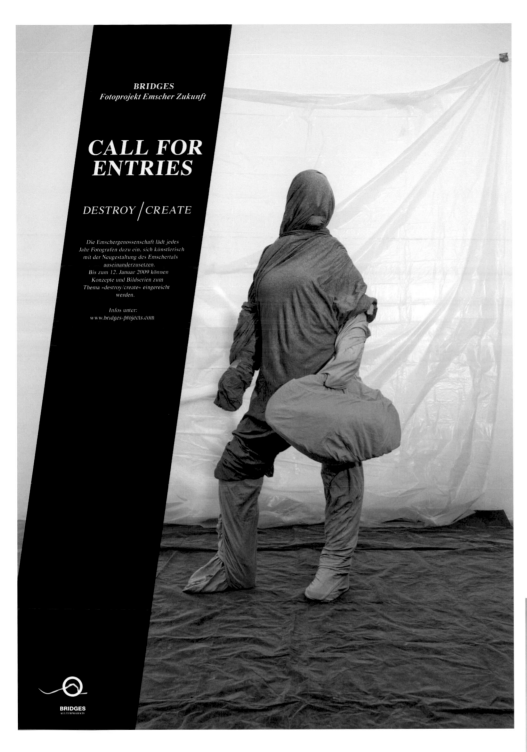

BUREAU MARIO LOMBARDO
Mario Lombardo

Emschergenossenschaft

Client Emschergenossenschaft
Credits Photography by Alfred Jansen, Markus Mrugalla / Art Direction by Mario Lombardo / Design by Catrin Sonnabend

page 0

R-Echos issue 1

Text: Electronest
Picture: by Amandine Alessandra
Art Direction: Electronest & Amandine Alessandra
Assistant: Owen Hoskins
Typography: Helvetica 72dpi
Production: &MP;

8pt _ abcdefghijklmnopqrstuvwxyz
ABCDEFGHIJKLMNOPQRSTUVWXYZ
01234567890

30pt _ abcdefghijklm
nopqrstuvwxyz
ABCDEFGHIJKLM
NOPQRSTUVWXYZ
01234567890

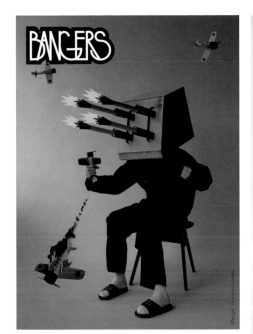

Design: studiospass.com

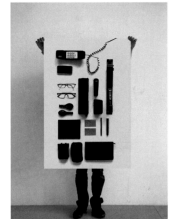

BURO RENG
[from left to right]

Pjuk

Balloon

Duo

—
ELECTRONEST
Jérôme Rigaud & Pierre Schmidt

[01]   R-Echos issue 1

(&MP - Ampersand Make Production)

Poster adressing the economics, production
and design by offering to become a share-
holder of the publication and investing in the
tangible production of a specific work.

Publisher &MP
Credits Photography by Amandine
Alessandra

—
STUDIOSPASS
Jaron Korvinus & Daan Mens

[02]   Boemklatsch: New BANGERS

Promotional flyer and poster series for
Bangers events at the cultural stage EKKO
in Utrecht.

Client EKKO and Jammm brands and entertainment, 2008–2009

[01]

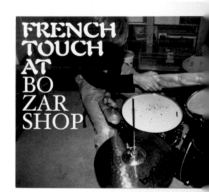

[02]

BASE DESIGN
Arno Baudin

[01] Bozarshop Identity

Design of identity for a Brussels-based
bookstore, which is a collaboration between Base, publisher Actar, architects
Lhoas&Lhoas, and Bozar itself, the Palais
des Beaux-Arts.

Client Bozarshop

NODE BERLIN OSLO

[02] Happy Days Sound Festival

Design for Happy Days Sound Festival 2005.
The series is also an homage to Kurt Schwit-
ters' sound poetry performed in Oslo.

Client Ny Musikk (Norwegian section of the International Society for Contemporary Music)
Credits Photography by Andreas Meichsner

STUDIO SPORT
Ronnie Fueglister

[03] Naga – A Forgotten Mountain
Region Rediscovered

Identity and signage for an exhibition at the
Museum der Kulturen Basel about the Naga
people, who are living in the border area
of Northeast India and Myanmar, a mountain area that has been sealed off for
many years.

Client / Publisher / Editor Museum der Kulturen Basel
Credits Photography by Milada Ganguli / Copyright
by Museum der Kulturen Basel

[01|02|03]

—
JOHAN PRAG

[01] Club 8 'The Boy Who Couldn't Stop Dreaming'
Client Avex

[02] The Back Horn 'Pulse'
Client Victor Entertainment, inc.

[03] Kahmi Karie 'Specialothers'
Client Victor Entertainment, Inc.

Album Covers.

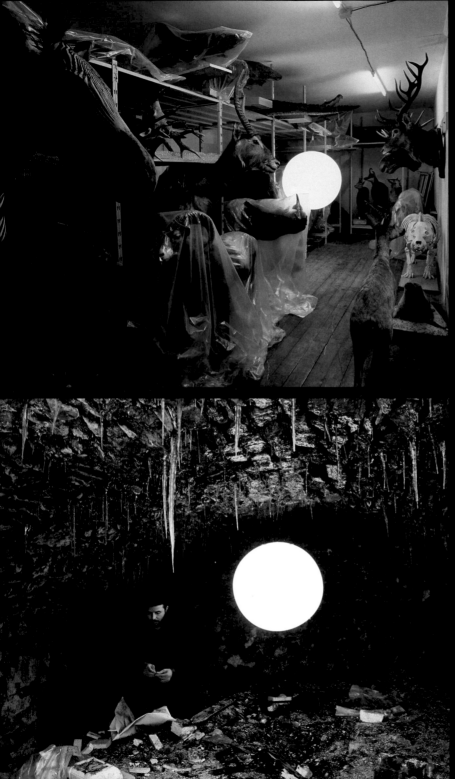

JAZZDOR
10.11–24.11.2006
FESTIVAL DE JAZZ DE STRASBOURG // 21ᵉ ÉDITION
TEL 03 88 36 30 48 // OFFENBURG 0761/822000 // WWW.JAZZDOR.COM

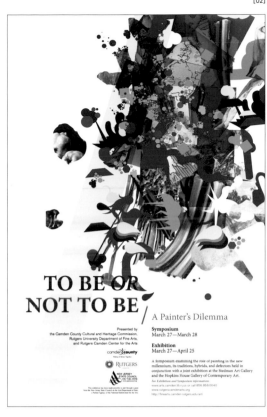

—
HELMO
Thomas Couderc & Clément Vauchez

[01]   JAZZDOR BERLIN 2009

Posters for two twin festivals.

Credits Photography by Daniel Erdmann and
Christophe Urbain

[03]   Colored Smoke

Work in progress as part of pictorial research
on smoke and coloured smoke.

—
GDLOFT

[02]   To Be or Not to Be: A Painter's Dilemma
Painting Symposium

Poster mailing designed to promote a
symposium focusing on issues surrounding
contemporary painting.

Client Rutgers University Camden Department
of Fine Arts
Editor Margery Amdur, Bruce Garrity
Credits Art direction by Allan Espiritu / Design by
Allan Espiritu, Laura Maryasz, Jamie Wagner

[03]

[01]

À 2 C'EST MIEUX

[01] Poggi Jewelry

Poggi is a Parisian brand of costume jewelry. For a glittering 2008 new year, we have decided to design a shield, set on discretely gold-textured paper.

Client / Credits Poggi

[02] La Surprise

Poster for the new communication agency of Théo Gennitsakis. The idea was to transpose the spirit of our atelier, with our friendly frog, the Wu-Tang or Nicolas de Staël, on the walls of Théo Gennitsakis' young company.

Client / Credits La Surprise / Théo Gennitsakis

[02]

[03]

TWOPOINTS.NET

[03] Creators Magazine

Poster and spread series for a magazine. The topic was rush hour in Barcelona.

Client Creators Magazine / Torras Papel

[04] Palau de la Música Catalana

Poster for the centennial of the *Palau De La Música Catalana* in Barcelona, an internationally known concert hall. The colourful Art Nouveau glass ceiling of the main concert hall served as the inspiration.

Client / Credits Palau de la Música Catalana

ERASE

The legibility of the contents is a key criterion in graphic design, and the conventional graphic designer should generally try to respect this. However, not doing what one should do also has its own aesthetic appeal, and designers who have mastered the form are entitled to break its rules. The rupture of visual codes in graphic design, which began in the 1990s with the use of ex-

tremely small fonts, is continued today with new characteristics. For example, where previously the most innovative and cutting edge font possible was used to present a certain message in a suitable visual manner, this trend has been reversed today: designers now use traditional and conventional fonts (e.g. Helvetica), and then disrupt legibility by using omissions, deletions and shifts as graphic design tools. The designers give the original content a very personal texture, which leads to increased attention from observers. Empty spaces awaken curiosity, and small deviations raise the question: "was this intentional or not?" In this way, the observer's perception is stimulated, and he or she must decipher the modified content by detecting what is missing, what is "wrong".

NEPOMUK

Artists in film

Posters for Berlin-based cinema. The posters are screen-printed by using a ciphering of the letters making the actual quote complete with an additional colour every week while making the past ones unreadable.

Client Cinema Babylon, Berlin
Publisher Kunsthochschule Berlin Weißensee
Credits Fonts by Berlin Park Display by Daniel Dolz/ Nepomuk and Thesis Sans/Serif

fig. 14

fig. 16

fig. 15

fig. 12

fig. 13

10

22

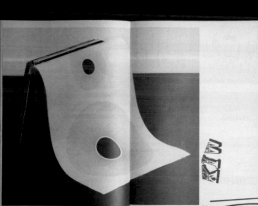

Rue de la Mouline 8
CH-1022 Chavannes-Près-Renens
Lausanne-ouest
Tél.: 021/691 41 50
Fax: 021/691 41 82

Horaires d'ouverture :
Lundi à vendredi : 9h-12h, 14h - 18h
Samedi : 9h-17h non-stop

Glory
LAND

Marché du seconde main

Le magasin Gloryland se situe dans la région de
l'ouest lausannois, à Chavannes.
Pendant un mois, un showroom y présente une
sélection d'objets représentatifs du magasin.

10.02.2009 – 13.03.2009

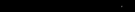

MATHIAS J. CLOTTU / ECAL

Gloryland

Catalogue of a showroom in Gloryland.

CONTAINERPLUS

Dream Story

Experimental piece based on Arthur Schnit-
zler's book titled *Dream Story*. By layering
different types of imagery that have been
subjected to a variety of processes — photocopied photography, drawing, splatters of
paint and layers of different paper, this
series of illustrations conjures up a mood
rather than depicts specific moments from
the narrative. This is a work in progress.

[01|02]

NOH Suntag
Ausnahmezustand / State of Emergency / 비상국가
1. März – 18. Mai 2008
Württembergischer Kunstverein Stuttgart

[03]

Landschaft (Entfernung)
31. März – 10. Juni 2007
Württembergischer Kunstverein Stuttgart

[04]

L2M3
Ina Bauer, Sascha Lobe

[01] NOH Suntag

[03] Landschaft – Entfernung

Posters for an exhibition at the Württemberg
Art Association

Client Württembergischer Kunstverein Stuttgart

MADS FREUND BRUNSE / ECAL

[02] Barsebäck

Poster regarding the artist's view on the
Swedish nuclear plant Barsebäck which is
situated at the border of Denmark. Made
using vapor in the development process in a
photolab, combined with radioactive types.

THEMES
Thomas Koenig

[04] Flying pizza: L'attaque Italienne

Poster presenting a live concert for a party
where the brand Prism sold a limited edition
T-shirt.

Client Prism

TATIANA RIHS
with assistance of Guillaume Chuard

[05] Poster for a contemporary art exhibition.

Client / Editor / Publisher Le Spectrarium
Credits Photography by © FLC / ADAGP, Paris 2008

METAHAVEN

[06] The Unresolved Borders of Europe

Empty envelope as a flyer for a lecture series
about the borders of the European Union.

Client NAiM / Bureau Europa, JVE, Maastricht

[05]

[06]

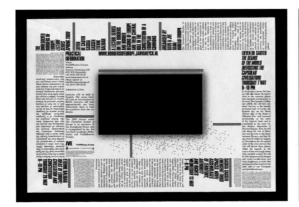
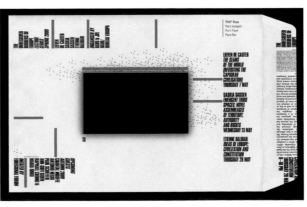

268

[01]

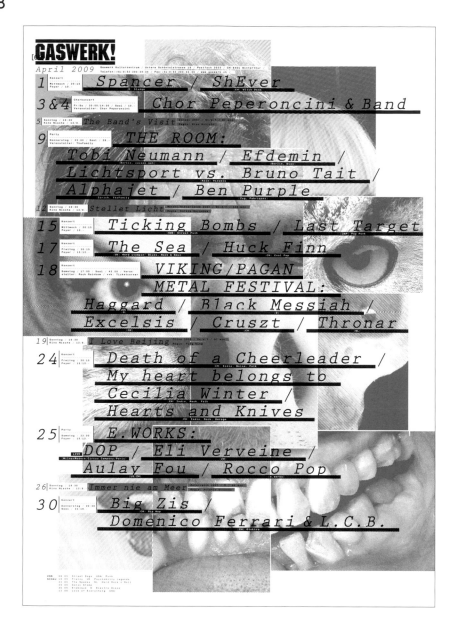

—
HI
Megi Zumstein & Claudio Barandun

[01–02]   Gaswerk Monthly Programm

Poster with monthly programme, each
time based on the same grid.

Client Kulturzentrum Gaswerk, Winterthur

—
CÔME DE BOUCHONY

[02]   Rawterdam

Poster.

—
ERICH BRECHBÜHL [MIXER]

[03]   Im Schtei Poster Series

Concert poster selection for the venue
Im Schtei.

Client Kulturkeller im Schtei

—
REMCO VAN BLADEL

[04]   By Method of Reasoning

Silkscreen poster for a publishing house.

Client / Publisher Onomatopee

[02]

[03|04]

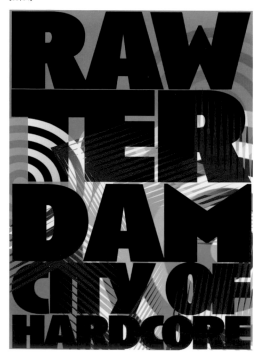

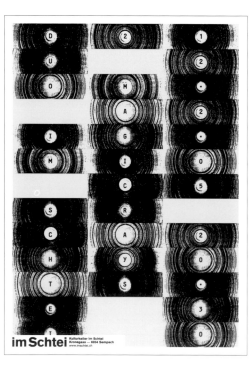

[01]

—
STUDIO SPORT
Ronnie Fueglister & Martin Stoecklin

[01] Plattform08

Identity and catalogue design for the second
issue of an exhibition project, showing a
selection of Switzerland's graduates in fine
art, photography and media art, curated by
young art historians.

Client / Publisher / Editor Kunstwollen Association

—
ABIABIABI
Abi Huynh

[02] 17x22, issue 3: headline

Poster vaguely parsing 16000 BBC breaking
news headlines over the course of one year.
Selected words were sorted by frequency,
creating a textual pattern.

[03] 17x22 issue 2: status

Poster focusing on the idea of "status", in
particular in Facebook Status Updates.

[04] Earth, map (excerpt)

Poster as a small excerpt from a larger map
project. This piece takes the idea of a map
and removes context and geographic association looking at the scale, content and
methodology of mapping.

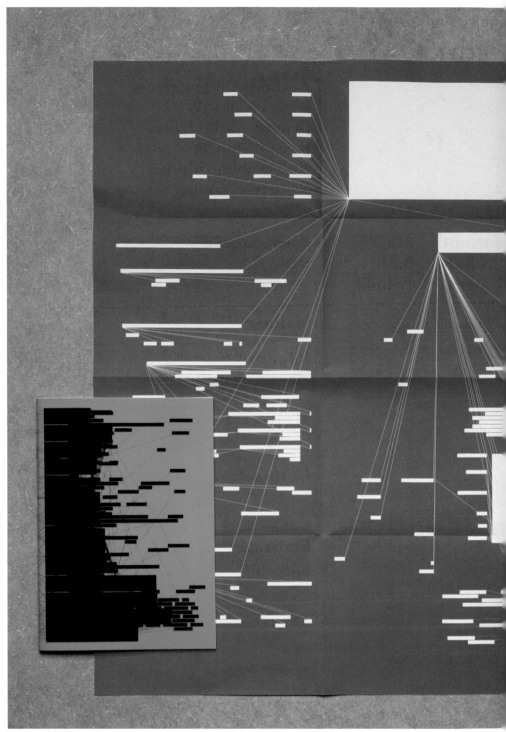

[02]

[03|04]

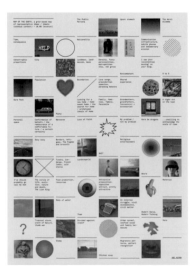

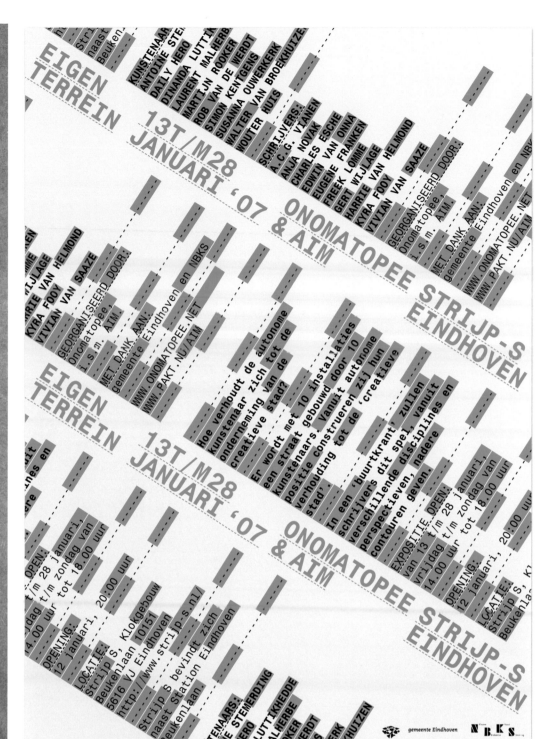

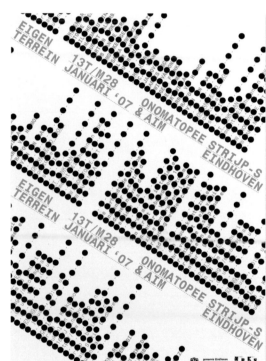

REMCO VAN BLADEL

Eigen Terrein

Client / Publisher Onomatopee

HANS GREMMEN / WYBERZEEFDRUK

Serendipity

Offset and Silkscreen posters designed by
coincidence. The artist made a selection
of 135 posters of which he compiled a book
called *Serendipity*. The book is about the
beauty of failure and serendipity.

Publisher Roma Publications

VELINA STOYKOVA

[01]   Cyanotype Poster

MARTIN NICOLAUSSON

[02]   No Cupcake Nor Proper Shoe

Poster for an exhibition focusing on the
space between word and image — eight
works were shown, combining poetry with
illustration.

Credits Text by Nina B. Stenberg

[02]

      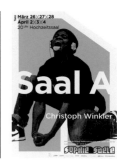

[01]

MILCHHOF : ATELIER

P. 274 – 275

Milchhof : atelier are: Hans Baltzer (b: 1972), Friedemann Bochow (b: 1975), Barbara Junge (b: 1972), Michael Rudolph (b: 1972), Carsten Stabenow (b: 1972) and Andreas Töpfer (b: 1971). While Stabenow grew up in Stralsund, Germany, the other five are from Berlin.

Describing themselves as a "community" and working side-by-side in their Berlin-based studio, the members of *milchhof : atelier* met while studying visual communication at Kunsthochschule Berlin-Weissensee, from where they graduated in 2000 and 2001. A collective of graphic designers, illustrators and artists, the five collaborate on projects they describe as being "connected with the cultural life of Berlin".

Of this work, they explain: "We try to develop a visual language for each project. For us, good design is achieved when content and shape match through humour, poetry and/or visual intelligence. For that purpose we are exploring all the possibilities that the discipline and its relative materials offer." "For example, for the *Tuned City project*, [a 2008 Berlin exhibition and conference which proposed a new evaluation of architectural spaces from the perspective of the acoustic], the printer was urged to change the five colour *Offset* inking system in every possible combination. This led to a series of over 25 different posters created within one printing process."

Clients to date include theatres: *Berliner Ensemble*, *Hebbeltheater*, *Saarländisches Staatstheater* and *Gorki Theatre*; electronic music festival *clubtransmediale*, urban open space designers *Topotek 1, Berlin City Council*, the Stumm Film Festival Berlin and stage, film and radio *publisher, Verlag Felix Bloch*.

[02]

MILCHHOF : ATELIER
Michael Rudolph, Andreas Töpfer

[03] Tuned City

Poster series for *Tuned City – Between sound and space speculation*, an exhibition and conference project proposing a new evaluation of architectural spaces from the perspective of the acoustic. The poster series was printed on a 5 colour offset machine loaded with 5 pantone special colours. The printer was allowed to play his Heidelberg printing machine like an instrument – switching the single colour units on and off in order to create a broad variety of overprint effects and many different posters at once.

^{Client} Tuned City

MILCHHOF : ATELIER
Michael Rudolph, Carsten Stabenow &
Andreas Töpfer

[01–02] Sophiensaele

Poster series for Berlin-based theatre. Each poster is a letter from the Sophiensaele logo.

^{Client} Sophiensaele Berlin

[03]

  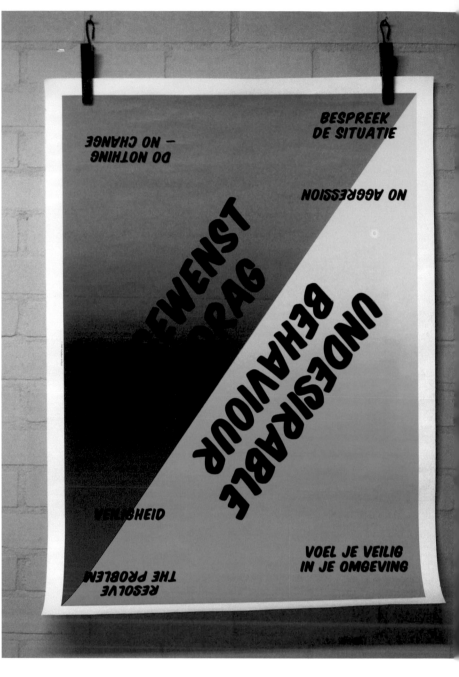

[01]

ALBAN SCHELBERT
& CHRISTOPHER WEST

[01] Undesirable Behaviour

Silkscreen posters and flyers for the Gerrit
Rietveld Academie's campain against undesirable behaviour at school.

Client / Publisher Gerrit Rietveld Academie

MARC BALLY / ECAL

[02] The Attic

Posters for concerts. For each event, the
design is overprinted on the club's corporate
paper, which is a perpetual calender. The
overprinting principle is used to announce
special guests, cancellations, reduced prices,
etc. It's also possible to recycle remaining
stocks of old posters.

KAREN VAN DE KRAATS

[03] Invitation Cream
PR Press days S/S 09 collections

Invite for the Spring/Summer collection of
a PR company. Each stack of 25 sheets had
a different combination of colours, and so
12 different invitations were defined. The design is copied black and white, and set in the
typeface Franklin Gothic Condensed Bold.

Client Cream PR
Editor Manuel Seikritt

[02]

[03]

[01]

SUPERBÜRO

[01] End::Spiel

Invitation posters for six improvised dance performances.

Client Susanne Mueller Nelson

DYNAMO
Thibaud Tissot

[02] French schoolbooks covers series

Covers series concept for the Neuchâtel secondary school's French schoolbooks. Graphic principle based on typographic mash-ups made of fragments from 5 differents fonts. The results implies the multiple faces of the French language as well as the appropriation of it by the student through the learning process.

Client State of Neuchâtel, Department of cultural affairs and public instruction

STUDIO OUTPUT
Dominic Prevost

[03] Saturday Sessions

Poster, flyer and advertisement for Ministry of Sound.

Client Ministry of Sound.

NA KIM

[04] Womenspeak!

Flyers for a series debate on feminism with art, politics, science and civil organizations. The identity of Womenspeak! varies in each event with the combination of different typefaces from Wonder Woman comics.

Client Tumult (NL)

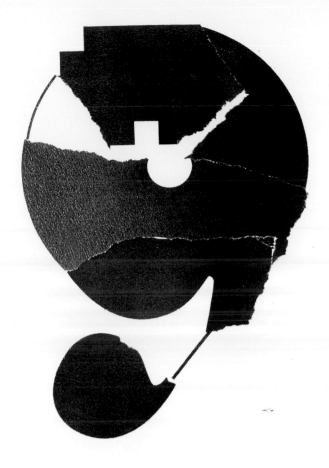

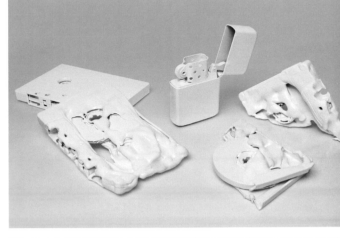

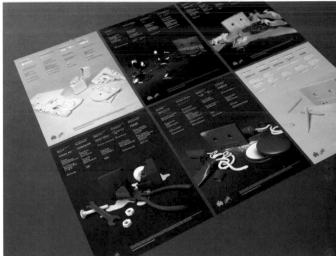

Women
SPEAK!
N° 1
Follow the leader
Kick-off nieuwe reeks WomenSpeak!
29.01.08, 8:00-9:30 pm
TUMULT, Domplein 5, Utrecht
Nancy Jouwe, Mira Kho,
Mariëlle Pals, Soula Notos &
Doreen Boonekamp e.a.b.

WOMEN SPEAK!
N° 4
Trots op homo's en lesbo's?
De Nederlandse leeuw
in een roze hemdje
15.06.08, 8:00-9:30 pm
TUMULT, Domplein 5, Utrecht
Ossama Abu Amar, Sarah Bracke,
Frank van Dalen,
Sooreh Hera & Markha Valenta

WOMEN SPEAK!
N° 5
Migrantenvrouwen:
de nieuwe globalisten
30.09.08, 8:00-9:30 pm
TUMULT, Domplein 4, Utrecht
Izaline Calister,
Stephanie Mbanzendore,
Fatumo Farah, Fenna Ulichki &
Joke van der Zwaard

GDLOFT

American Institute of Graphic Arts,

Philadelphia Design Competition Catalogue

Catalogue design for American Institute of
Graphic Arts, Philadelphia Design Competition. The catalog print-run was limited to
the same number of entries received (576)
to represent all the work of the design
community. Using a variable printing program, each cover is a different colour of a
predetermined spectrum. Each catalog was
individually numbered.

Client American Institute of Graphic Arts,
Philadelphia
Editor Dr. Joseph Schiavo
Credits Art direction by Allan Espiritu / Design by
Allan Espiritu, Laura Maryasz, Jamie Wagner
Photography by Matt Bednarik / Texts by Michele
Cooper, Allan Espiritu, Dr. Joseph Schiavo Design
Interns Laura Maryasz, Bill Engles

DAVID ISAKSSON, ANDERS LÖVGREN,
MARTIN NICOLAUSSON, JONAS NORDIN

[01]   Beckmans College of Design graduation show

Posters

Client Beckmans College of Design

FILIP KLEREMARK

[02]   Rollerboys Recordings EP's
[03]   Bogdan Irkük – The Distant EP
[04]   Ultracity – Swetalic EP

Record sleeve design for the label Rollerboy
Recordings.

[01]

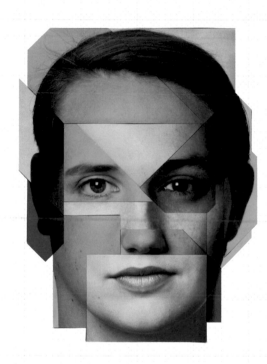

[02|03|04]

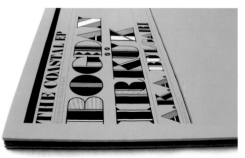

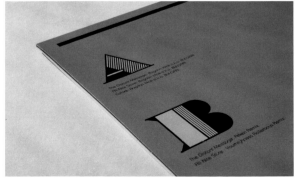

INDEX
M – Z

REGULAR
GRAPHIC
DESIGN
TODAY

Edited by Robert Klanten, Sven Ehmann & Adeline Mollard
Preface by François Rappo
Introduction by Robert Klanten
Profile Texts by Roanne Bell

Cover and Layout by Adeline Mollard for Gestalten
Typeface: AS Black Medium & Light by © Aurèle Sack (www.a--s.ch)

Project management by Elisabeth Honerla for Gestalten
Production management by Janine Milstrey for Gestalten
Production assistance by Natalie Reed for Gestalten
Translation by Patrick Sheehan
Proofreading and translation preface by Joseph Pearson
Printed by C&C Offset Printing, China

Published by Gestalten, Berlin 2009
ISBN 978-3-89955-253-9

For more information, please check www.gestalten.com

Bibliographic information published by the Deutsche Nationalbibliothek.
The Deutsche Nationalbibliothek lists this publication in the Deutsche
Nationalbibliografie; detailed bibliographic data is available on
the internet at http://dnb.d-nb.de.

None of the content in this book was published in exchange for payment
by commercial parties or designers; Gestalten selected all included work
based solely on its artistic merit.

This book was printed according to the internationally accepted ISO
14001 standards for environmental protection, which specify require-
ments for an environmental management system. It has been printed
on PEFC certified paper which ensures responsible paper sources with
sustainable forest management.

Gestalten is a climate neutral company and so are our products.
We collaborate with the non-profit carbon offset provider myclimate
(www.myclimate.org) to neutralize the company's carbon footprint
produced through our worldwide business activities by investing in
projects that reduce CO_2 emissions (www.gestalten.com/myclimate).